USING SIMULATIONS TO PROMOTE
LEARNING IN HIGHER EDUCATION

ENHANCING LEARNING SERIES

EDITORS: John P. Hertel and Barbara J. Millis

USING SIMULATIONS TO PROMOTE LEARNING IN HIGHER EDUCATION

An Introduction

John P. Hertel
Barbara J. Millis

STERLING, VIRGINIA

Published in 2002 by

Stylus Publishing, LLC
22883 Quicksilver Drive
Sterling, Virginia 20166

Library of Congress Cataloging-in-Publication Data

Hertel, John P., 1948–
    Using simulations to promote learning in higher education:
an introduction/John P. Hertel and Barbara J. Millis.—1st ed.
        p. cm. — (Enhancing learning series)
    Includes bibliographical references and index.
    ISBN 1-57922-052-5 (pbk: alk. paper)
    1. Education—Simulation methods. 2. Experiential learning.
3. College teaching. I. Millis, Barbara J. II. Title. III. Series.
    LB1029.S53 H48 2002
    378.1'797—dc21   2001057696

First edition, 2002
ISBN: paperback 1-57922-052-5
Printed in the United States of America

All first editions printed on acid-free paper

For me, this book began more than 10 years ago as a post-J.D. student in a semester-long capstone course at George Washington University's National Law Center. Professor James M. Brown, who had mastered simulation teaching, taught this remarkable course. I became fascinated. For the next 5 years, I did what I could to assist Jim with the course, and in return he mentored me in its design and administration. One semester we developed and ran a 1-day simulation in another course. It was exciting to see students learn substantive law by simulating roles in an actual legal case during a 2-hour class. Later, we designed a simulation scenario based on a complex environmental case that was being played for real by several branches of the federal government, the State of North Carolina, and private commercial interests. We used real-life players in this 2-day simulation at a U.S. Marine Corps wargaming center. The exercise opened eyes and propelled participants years ahead in negotiations.

These experiences convinced me of the effectiveness of the simulation method of teaching. At George Washington University, I saw law students without a day of experience "practice law" with more intensity and sophistication than they could acquire in a year's worth of clerking in a law office. In North Carolina, I saw experienced attorneys and seasoned professionals test their positions against the law and real political interests. In both cases, participants learned substantive legal principles and processes, developed legal skills, and worked together to further individual (role) interests. They learned to manage time, to meet deadlines, and to balance competing interests. Most important, they learned how to interact with others to *apply* what they had learned.

What was missing was a guide to help others use this method of teaching, in and out of academia. Professor Brown had been doing this so long it was second nature to him. He could "feel" his students' critical mass of activity building and solve problems before they occurred (or wisely allow them to occur). But he had never dissected his pedagogy to the point of being able to tell someone else how to use it.

Like you, I have "reinvented the wheel" enough times to know its frustration. Conversely, I have adapted others' successes to my needs enough to have had satisfying careers as both a practicing attorney and an undergraduate professor. It is my sincere hope—and Professor Brown's deserved legacy—that after reading this book you will decide to give it a try. Its methods are adaptable to most academic disciplines. Once you try this method of teaching, you and your students will be hooked . . . because it is fun and it works.

John P. Hertel

My dedication is far simpler: To my beloved family, especially my daughter, Jeanne, who is reinforcing for me during her teenage years the power of patience and love. And, to my in-laws, Jack and Jean Millis, whom I have known since I was 17. They have brought us constant wisdom and joy since moving to Colorado Springs.

Barbara J. Millis

CONTENTS

I hear and I forget
I see and I remember
I do and I understand
—Chinese Proverb

This book is for teachers who are looking for new ways to enhance student learning. It is for teachers who are curious about simulation teaching and for those who are familiar with the concepts but have not yet joined faculty who are using them in their classes. It is for teachers who have successfully used games and seek to go deeper into experiential learning with their students. It is for teachers who have used others' simulations and want to know how to design and implement their own. And last, it is for experienced teachers who are convinced that simulations fulfill an important teaching need and want to expand their creative use of simulations.

Simulations have no agreed-upon definitions, even as used in higher education. There are several generally accepted characteristics of education simulations, however, which we explain. As we discuss their educational value, we *describe* rather than define what we mean by an education simulation. The simulations we discuss are not "off-the-shelf" generic exercises to play in class such as Bafa Bafa or The Prisoner's Dilemma, nor are they electronic constructs such as Sim City. Rather, this book is written to help you design and use your own simulations. Thus, it will enhance your students' learning in your specific discipline—its substantive content, skills, and processes, and its application to the world your students will join upon graduation.

Beyond design, we explain all aspects of using education simulations in class. However, we caution you not to get bogged down with these mechanics at the outset. Instead, first read through enough of the two initial chapters to get to a comfortable level of understanding education simulations. Then, if you become as excited as we did, dive into the next few chapters to learn how to design, manage, debrief, and assess simulations in your class. Chapter 7 and the appendixes offer specific examples of an extended multiscenario simulation that you are welcome to adapt to your course. This final chapter explains how to integrate several substantive topics, skills, or both to serve as a capstone course to bridge the gap between professional education and practice. We hope and expect that you will tab, dog-ear, or put sticky notes or fingers at certain pages of this book while you go back and forth between chapters to learn the ins and outs of education simulations.

Simulations are fun and motivating to use—for students and teachers. We hope your reading of our book is the same.

John P. Hertel
Barbara J. Millis

I

WHY SIMULATIONS FURTHER EDUCATIONAL GOALS

"Not only did I learn more substantive law than in any other course I've taken," declared an "alumnus" of a legal simulation course, "but I learned why I needed to learn all of those things." Such take-aways emphasize the value of using simulations in undergraduate and graduate programs. Using education simulations weaves substance-specific information into real-life problems in meaningful ways that students can understand.

Although education simulations can creatively focus on experimentation, prediction, and evaluation (Cunningham, 1984), we concentrate on the general educational goals of (a) transfer of knowledge, (b) skill development, and (c) the application of both knowledge and skills. During a simulation students typically acquire broad discipline-specific knowledge that they are able to later transfer into a professional setting. Simulations also "teach" much more, including the processes involved in the discipline; the organizations involved; and the interactions with other disciplines, people, and organizations. As we hope to make clear, education simulations are particularly valuable for integrating different teaching objectives, whether they be coalescing different principles or bringing together substantive knowledge with specific practice skills. These multifaceted features make simulations powerful pedagogical tools for integrated courses or capstone course, especially the extended simulations we describe in chapter 7.

Motivation

Greenblat (1981) identifies four key elements involved in getting students to learn from simulations:

> (1) We need to find modes of creating motivation prior to transmitting information; (2) the learner must be an active participant in the learning process, rather than a passive recipient of information; (3) instruction must be individualized such that learning is at the appropriate pace for each learner; (4) there must be prompt feedback on success and error. (p. 17)

Teachers who have used simulations overwhelmingly agree that this method of learning *motivates* the students. Theall and Franklin (1999), after editing a book examining motivation as it relates to teaching, learning, and institutional programs, found convergence in the current research on motivation. They found a "consistent pattern of emphasis on a group of six factors: inclusion, attitude, meaning, competence, leadership, and satisfaction" (p. 105). All of these factors are apparent in well-organized simulations. Interestingly enough, with a simulation, the instructor shares leadership responsibilities with students, allowing them to assume roles that would be nonexistent in a traditionally taught class. This approach fosters what Finkel (2000) called "inquiry-based learning." To motivate students, he recommended designing courses, like a simulation, as an inquiry into a problem:

> In a course called *Political Ecology* students learn large chunks of economics and biology as they wrestle with the

problem of reconciling economic prosperity and environmental protection. In *Health: Individual and Community,* they master parts of biology, psychology, anthropology, and sociology in their attempt to discover whether or not there are new ways to conceive of health care.

Such a shift changes everything. To teach such a course the teacher first must have a problem—one that will interest students, and that also interests him. Once he has the problem he can then launch the investigation. It is from the investigation, the attempt to solve the problem, that learning will flow. *If the students are interested in the inquiry, then they will want to learn whatever is necessary to pursue that inquiry.* No extrinsic reasons for learning need to be offered no pie in the sky invoked. (p. 55)

All researchers who have looked at motivation agree that it cannot be "imposed" on students. They have to somehow get "fired up."

Fortunately, active learning can play a key role in motivating students. Emphasizing Greenblat's (1981) second element, the entire structure of a simulation class is built around the concept of students *participating* in a variety of roles within an environment designed around the learning objectives of the course. Petranek, Corey, and Black (1992) concluded that this participatory interaction helps students learn through education simulations: "During a simulation participants unconsciously process all types of information: facts, emotions, strategies, outcomes, relationships, feelings, and much more. . . . Learning happens because the students are active and not passive in the process. They are able to experiment with various options and interact with fellow students" (p. 176). Active participation and relevance to the real world tends to foster motivation, although, as Orbach (1979) pointed out, initial motivations—prompted by the challenge of the simulation itself—can lead to active participation. He concluded, "Active participation in simulation games is not a cause of motivation but rather the result of it. Without motivation in the first place, there would be no active participation in the second" (p. 7). Thus, Greenblat's elements are closely linked: To put it poetically in the words of William Butler Yeats, "You can't separate the dancer from the dance."

Deep Learning

The research on the value of active learning and participation is definitive. International studies suggest that it can lead to deep learning. A project, "Improving Student Learning," sponsored by the Council for National Academic Awards in Britain, was initiated not to generate new research about student learning but rather to encourage faculty to use the existing research and tools to strengthen their courses. The project is predicated on research indicating:

> The students' approach to learning—whether they take a surface or a deep approach—[is] the crucial factor determining the quality of learning outcomes. Those who take a deep approach understand more, produce better written work containing logical structures and conclusions rather than lists, remember longer, and obtain better marks and degrees than those students who take a surface approach. (as cited in "Deep Learning, Surface Learning," 1993, p. 14)

Rhem (1995a, 1995b) cited three international scholars (Ference Marton [Sweden], Noel Entwistle [Scotland], and Paul Ramsden [Australia]) who, with other colleagues, have identified the same emergent patterns in deep learning. This research suggests that although specific implementations will vary, four key components characterize a deep, rather than a surface, approach to learning. Rhem (1995b) summarized them as follows:

> Motivational context: We learn best what we feel a need to know. Intrinsic motivation remains inextricably bound to some level of choice and control. Courses that remove these take away the sense of ownership and kill one of the strongest elements in lasting learning.

Learner Activity: Deep learning and "doing" travel together. Doing in itself isn't enough. Faculty must connect activity to the abstract conceptions that make sense of it, but passive mental postures lead to superficial learning.

Interaction with others: As Noel Entwistle put it in a recent email message, "The teacher is not the only source of instruction or inspiration." Peers working as groups enjoin dimensions of learning that lectures and readings by themselves cannot touch.

A well-structured knowledge base: This doesn't just mean presenting new material in an organized way. It also means engaging and reshaping the concepts students bring with them when they register. Deep approaches, learning for understanding, are integrative processes. The more fully new concepts can be connected with students' prior experience and existing knowledge, the more likely it is they will be impatient with inert facts and eager to achieve their own synthesis. (p. 4)

This research has enormous implications for college and university teaching. Researchers generally agree, for example, that group work and problem solving within the context outlined above can result in deep learning. Thus, simulations become a powerful tool for learning.

As Greenblat (1981) also emphasized, the *pace of an education simulation* is important, which is why we recommend several methods for managing the dissemination of information and role interaction later in this book. While sharing with internships, clinics, and service learning the advantages of real-world experiences, simulations have several practical and educational advantages over these "real-time" teaching methods. By designing the simulation without all of the complexities and distractions of real life, students are able to focus on the instructor's intended learning objectives. Instructors can also "design out" negative learning experiences that often occur in actual practice. Thus, students in an education simulation can take risks without fear of harm to real people or real events, and they are free to learn from mistakes.

Simulations promote student motivation and participation because events can unfold and decisions can be made at an accelerated pace. Furthermore, irrelevant time-consuming events can be condensed or eliminated. Allowing students to replay their activities after debriefing earlier actions gives both students and teachers unparalleled opportunities to apply different approaches to the same problems. And, because each student has an assigned role in the scenario action, instruction is also individualized.

For the same reason, *feedback is also individualized*. Feedback—including each graded event—can be a powerful impetus for learning. Woods (1996) emphasized that "the key issue is to assess students so that they learn what we want them to learn: so that they acquire the behaviours we desire as outcomes of the program" (p. 5-1). Providing feedback is a complex process. Bransford, Brown, and Cocking (2000) acknowledged the value of feedback to learning but emphasized that it is not a "unidimensional concept." Feedback on memorization differs significantly from feedback related to understanding: "Students need feedback about the degree to which they know when, where, and how to use the knowledge they are learning" (Bransford et al., 2000, p. 59). This in-depth, applied feedback is a key value of simulations. Much of it occurs, as we discuss later, in debriefing the simulation. Additionally, as later chapters emphasize, particularly chapter 6, feedback can be both prompt and frequent throughout the simulation experience.

Other learning theories support the use of simulations. For example, Burns and Gentry (1998) wrote about the "tension-to-learn" theory for experiential learning. This theory "holds that the learner passes through the following phases: (a) current state, (b) motivation, (c) experience, (d) legitimization, and (e) new state" (p. 141). Once again, simulation instruction intentionally follows these phases of learning, and the tension Burns and Gentry wrote of is intentionally designed into the simulation scenarios. As we hope to make clear, the unique manner of creating student interactions (with the substance of their course, with the processes of their discipline, and with each other) creates a meaningful experience. The simulation debriefing as well as the interactions throughout the simulation provide the legitimization necessary to bring the students to the new state of knowledge and experience. In an extended simulation, such as the one described in chapter 7, most students actually cycle through these phases several times during the course.

Educational theories on adult learning, particularly those focused on the nontraditional learners entering modern classrooms in record numbers, also support the use of simulations. Traditional students are now a minority on many campuses. Students often tend to be older part-timers balancing academic demands with work and family obligations. With this diverse student population, Gaff (1992) emphasized that, "pedagogical 'business-as-usual' in any program—listening to lectures, reading a pre-digested textbook, memorization, and multiple-choice tests—will not allow students to learn what even the most fervently argued courses have to teach" (p. 35). Learning will not take place with "authority figures" lecturing to passive adults. In fact, as Giezkowski (1992) pointed out, the large influx of adult students into colleges and universities—because they are focused and pragmatic and bring with them a wealth of life experiences—has often revitalized the learning environment. Because most simulation-based classes involve more mature students, instructors should be reassured by the research by Simpson (1980) that "the two distinguishing characteristics of adult learning most frequently advanced by theorists are the adult's autonomy of direction in the act of learning and the use of personal experience as a learning resource" (p. 25).

Dentler (1994), a community college history teacher, also pointed out that many teachers have radically different backgrounds from the students they teach:

Our students, shaped by far different academic, economic, personal, and political experiences, typically do not feel empowered in the classroom. They are alienated from institutions, including colleges, that too often serve to heighten their sense of exclusion from positions of power and privilege in society. Most importantly, our students do not have the self-esteem required to confidently participate in competition-based class discussion that follows the traditional passive-learning lecture methods. (p. 12)

She concluded:

When we ask our urban community college students to find answers on their own and share them, non-competitively, with their classmates, we empower them in a way that wasn't even necessary for my generation of college students. When our students work with their peers on research projects . . . we are literally inviting them to participate in the system. For many, this is the first time the system has welcomed them at the table. (p. 12)

Simulations thus can be powerful tools for integrating students into a system that may be foreign to their prior experiences.

These issues do not touch only community college instructors. A scientist, Nelson (1996), from a large research institution, thought earlier that diversity issues had little or no effect on his teaching of biological topics. He now thinks differently:

Subsequently, I have come to understand that much of what I took as neutral teaching practice actually functions to keep our courses less accessible to students from non-traditional backgrounds. If my current understandings are a reasonable reflection of reality, then (almost) all traditionally taught courses are unintentionally but nevertheless deeply biased in ways that make substantial differences in performance for many students. (p. 165)

Among other pedagogical approaches, Nelson suggests "a shift to structured, student-student group work" with the caveats that "the teacher must make sure that the students are prepared for the discussion, that the students participate constructively and fairly evenly, and that the students are addressing questions that are sufficiently challenging" (p. 167). Simulations address all of these critical issues, and more.

Achieve Learning Objectives

First and foremost, education simulations are designed around the instructor's learning objectives. Following some of the same phases Burns and Gentry (1998) mentioned, Gosen and Wash-bush (1999) made the case that the pedagogical tools employed have a profound impact on learning outcomes. Astin's (1993) comprehensive longitudinal study of the effect of college on undergraduate students reinforces this significant conclusion. Using samples from 159 baccalaureate-granting institutions, Astin investigated 22 outcomes affected by 88 environmental factors to determine influences on students' academic achievement, personal development, and satisfaction with college. He determined that two factors in particular, student-student interaction and student-faculty interaction, carried the largest weights and affected the largest number of general education outcomes. Because of the influence of peers and faculty, he concluded that "how students *approach* general education (and how the faculty actually *deliver* the curriculum) is far more important than the formal curricular content and structure" (p. 425).

Thus, based on solid pedagogical grounds, Gosen and Wash-bush (1999) used simulations to help their business students integrate their educational experiences to accomplish these six clear goals:

1. Use what they have learned in their common core courses to accurately and coherently describe company situations.

2. Use facts from real or case situations and identify relevant crucial strategic issues worthy of management concern.

3. Develop skills of structuring and presenting arguments that can logically persuade management to follow action recommendations.

4. Propose actions to logically and effectively contend with problems identified.

5. Participate as a member of a strategic management team in a simulated business environment.

6. Make and stand accountable for management decisions made in a simulated business environment. (p. 294)

This focus on learning objectives or goals requires a carefully thought-out course syllabus. Instructors should, for example, include clear explanations about the nature, purpose, and value of simulations in their course syllabi. Brookfield (1991) warned:

> Being clear about why you teach is crucial, but it is not enough in and of itself; you must also be able to communicate to your students the values, beliefs, and purposes comprising your rationale. You cannot assume that students will understand your rationale or be immediately convinced that your most deeply held convictions have value for them as well. (p. 22)

Brookfield's cautions emphasize the research on deep learning cited at the opening of this chapter. The quality of student learning, Ramsden (cited in Rhem, 1995b) stated, is dependent on two things: (a) the reasons you use specific teaching and assessment methods and (b) the way your students perceive them. The latter is the most important. He stressed, "The key thing to understand about approaches is that they arise from the student's *perception* of the teacher's requirements" (cited in Rhem, 1995b, p. 4). Faculty must consciously foster these perceptions to build student buy-in for simulations. Instructors thus should conscientiously prepare syllabi defining simulations, explaining the rationale for their use, and explicitly laying out classroom procedures.

Such a syllabus cannot be perfunctory, providing only a partial snapshot of the course. An enriched syllabus (Gabennesch, 1992) does not, like a lecture, direct canned information in one direction. It invites students, instead, to join a mutual conversation. This conversation, as Duffy and Jones (1995) suggested, "introduces a learning community into the classroom environment. It unites the professor and the students in a documented conversation, and in this way it holds both professor and students accountable for that classroom community" (p. 69).

We agree with Jones (1987) and others who criticize an approach to education, sometimes inadvertently fostered by state-mandated assessments, that depends on a step-to-step transfer of facts that can be easily quantified by objective and frequent testing. Education—particularly higher education—should be designed on the basis of application of knowledge, interaction with ideas and people, experience, feedback, and reflection. Simulations are structured precisely on these premises.

Student-Centered Learning

We also see learning as a process, during which there is a change in the learner. "Change" can be defined in different ways, depending on the discipline approach. Leamnson (1999), for instance, looked at learning as a biological occurrence common to all human beings. He recommended a shift to student-centered learning because student brains are the ones that need to change. College and university professors who prepare "brilliant" lectures have modified and strengthened their own brain synapses, but the impact on students is less clear. He concluded:

> The only hopeful position a college teacher can take is to believe that axons continue to bud in the brains of their students, and that new and potentially useful synapses are forming, and that these synapses will, if everyone does the right things, stabilize and strengthen, and learning will take place. (p. 21)

Simulations, which leave information gathering, the key decisions, and the conclusions in the hands—and minds—of the students can therefore result in significant learning.

Also, because students each learn differently, at different paces, simulations allow instructors to deal with this individual learning more systematically.

Increasing students' knowledge is an important goal of all education, but simulations are particularly adept at helping students acquire usable knowledge, that is, knowledge that can transfer and be applied to other situations. Cunningham (1984) pointed out, "Most educational simulations are designed based on the assumption that learning involves a transfer of knowledge and a change in behavior. Learning is not simply the storage of information, but the ability to use it (p. 224). Bransford et al. (2000) related this understanding to deep learning: "Deep understanding of subject matter transforms factual information into usable knowledge" (p. 16). Simulations encourage the purposeful use of knowledge to achieve clearly defined goals, according to Petranek et al. (1992): "During a game [or simulation] a student has not merely to learn some information, but has to fit it into a social structure in order to achieve a particular goal" (p. 175). Simulations therefore become powerful tools for developing student competence in the designated areas of inquiry, whether they be business, law, biology, accounting, or any other discipline.

Bridging the Gap(s)

Education simulations can also help bridge the gaps between disciplines. Education simulations provide unique structures for integrating substantive principles as well as doctrines and skills. This capability makes them particularly useful for capstone courses that attempt to bring together the essential learning objectives of multiple courses within an academic or professional discipline. By themselves, or in conjunction with other traditional teaching methods, simulations should be considered as a central structure around which a capstone course evolves. Experienced educators conclude that students "find it enlightening to apply ideas and concepts from their many courses to the simulation at hand" (Petranek et al., 1992, p. 176).

Another particularly important use of simulations in education is to facilitate efforts at what has become known as "bridging the gap" between the academics of a profession and the practice of that profession (law, health care, accounting, teaching, etc.). Simulations are ideal for connecting factual knowledge, principles, and skills to their application within a profession. They help students understand the environment and processes of a profession in a way that other teaching methods cannot. They provide students with an opportunity for decision making, and for evaluating the consequences of their decisions that no textbook or laboratory can. Bransford et al. (2000) concluded that "to develop competence in an area of inquiry, students must: (a) have a deep foundation of factual knowledge, (b) understand facts and ideas in the context of a conceptual framework, and (c) organize knowledge in ways that facilitate retrieval an application" (p. 16).

Jones (1987) emphasized through an analogy that education simulations can be used differently for different purposes. Children "play doctor" just for the fun of it. Other people replicate a doctor's life just to see what it is like. Medical students simulate doctors in a professional setting to test their substantive knowledge and skills or to get the "feel" of a hospital environment, providing them with a controlled experience on which they can build additional learning. Whatever your purpose in teaching, if you use education simulations, you must remember to tell your students not to "act like doctors," but to "be doctors." In a controlled environment, simulations allow students to "be" that doctor or lawyer or accountant.

A separate argument for why you should consider using simulations in your course focuses on the "other" necessary participant in every educational endeavor—the teacher. We have already noted that, in a simulation course, the teacher must at least share responsibility for learning with the students, and in some cases give up that responsibility completely. Simulation teachers become guides in a journey of learning. They facilitate changes in behavior, and thereby the learning, of their students. They cause their students to learn, which is the reason they are teachers. Furthermore, they find themselves able to explore topics of interest in greater depth. Finkel (2000) in a course predicated on inquiry-centered teaching saw himself addressing the same questions as his students. He noted, however, a "plus" for all teachers who model lifelong learning: "My inquiry was not at the same level as those of my students; I had a head start on them" (p. 58).

All of these are reasons why simulations clearly further educational goals. But the one we like the best was offered by Gibbs (1978) when discussing using games in education, "I have operated on the simple principle that if there is a possible educational benefit to be derived from a game it should be included" (p. 2). Based on our own experiences using simulations in the classroom, we agree completely.

2

WHAT IS AN EDUCATION SIMULATION?

Describing an Education Simulation

Educators have been designing, using, evaluating, and writing about simulations for more than 40 years. However, there are no generally accepted definitions of an education simulation or its many variations. As we use the term, education simulations are sequential decision-making classroom events in which students fulfill assigned roles to manage discipline-specific tasks within an environment that models reality according to guidelines provided by the instructor. Throughout this book we offer other authors' descriptions of simulations, enabling you to form your own idea of what a simulation is and whether it will help you to teach your students in any of the ways we discussed in chapter 1.

Although Gibbs (1978), who published a dictionary of games and simulations, and others have attempted to catalog all the various permutations of simulations, games, role playing, and other interactive, experiential pedagogies, we are staying clear of these semantic debates. We do agree with Jones (1987), however, that you should not try to force an education simulation too hard into a dictionary definition that suggests imitation, mimicry, or unreality—although some of those elements apply. Education simulations typically place students in true-to-life roles, and although the simulation activities are "real world," modifications occur for learning purposes.

Similarly, because of the element of unreality, we distinguish between simulations and games. Like simulations, games can be effective learning tools, but some key characteristics distinguish them from simulations. For instance, unlike education simulations, games often involve elements of fantasy and make-believe. Furthermore, the rules of play in games are likely to be fixed and rigid, unlike the more fluid and often spontaneous guidelines of simulations. Finally, many academic games, such as variations of bingo, are predicated on a combination of knowledge and luck. The luck factor gives all students, even the less able, a chance to win, thus increasing motivation. In simulations, the actions of the players typically have more predictable outcomes and luck brings no greater chance of success than it does in real life. Although games can also effectively reinforce or increase knowledge or strengthen skills, in the classroom they typically do so through less complex methods than simulations. Often the learning objectives are less clear-cut in games.

Following Jones's (1987) lead, we also steer clear of what he calls the "hyphenated horrors," terms such as simulation-games, simulation-exercises, simulation-events, gaming-simulations, and so on. As Gertrude Stein once quipped, "A rose by any other name would smell as sweet." The use to which a teacher puts a teaching technique is more important than what the technique is called. Birnbaum (1982) also emphasized the use to which simulations are put: "Games and simulations are another curricular approach to the problem of providing students with realistic situations structured to reveal significant interactions that lead to focused learning objectives established by a faculty member" (p. 4). So, we focus on *describing* rather than defining simulations and on discussing their uses.

Most effective teachers begin to build their courses by deciding what their learning objectives will be. This book focuses on how to design, manage, debrief, and assess simulations to achieve higher education learning objectives.

In the most general sense, a simulation involves people, an environment, and activities. These three components can be broken down to one more level. The people are the students and the teacher. The environment consists of the simulation itself—which in briefer examples consists of a single scenario but in an extended version may contain multiple interwoven scenarios—and the rules. The rules relate both to the simulation environment in which the actors play and to the class where the students are members. And the activities consist of those that prepare students for participation in the simulation, those that are related to the conduct of the simulation itself, and those that foster the debriefing stage. We explain all of these components later.

As indicated earlier, simulations are based on reality. However, these models of real-world situations contain only those parts of reality that the designer/educator considers relevant to previously identified learning objectives. Greenblat (1981) put this well:

> Simulation, then, entails abstraction and representation from a larger system. Central features must be identified and simplified, while less important elements are omitted from the model. It is the very process of highlighting some elements and eliminating others that makes the model useful. (p. 22)

In almost all cases this model is both simplified and accelerated in terms of issues, participants, time, decision-making forums, and process procedures. Simplifying them makes them effective for learning. Deciding what to keep and what to eliminate is the job of the simulation designer and the teacher. The careful planning results in a simulation that meets the teacher's learning objectives.

Structure of Education Simulations

In chapters 3 and 7 we discuss elements of some models you can use to design a simulation for the classroom. We feel the same way about simulation models that we do about definitions—there is no universally accepted standard for them. There are, however, several common features or characteristics of an education simulation model. The more familiar you are with them, the more capably you can design your own simulation to help you to teach—and your students to learn—your course knowledge and skills. Appendixes A–C offer some simulation models with these features. We suggest that you at least glance at these examples to become familiar with our models. Better yet, put a thumb in the appendix while reading the following sections. And, if it helps you here, keep your thumb there while reading chapters 3, 4, and 5.

As with definitions, various educator/authors have developed their own lists of the structural characteristics of a simulation model. Ruben and Lederman (1982) classified the characteristics of experienced-based instructional activities as: "(1) participants cast in roles; (2) interactions between those roles; (3) rules governing the interactions; (4) goals with respect to which interactions occur; and (5) criteria for determining the attainment of the goals and the termination of the activity" (p. 235). Gredler (1992) believed that the fundamental features of simulations are the interactions between participants and the simulation elements and among the participants. She listed what she considers to be the five basic characteristics of simulations:

- Simulations are problem-based units of learning that are set in motion by a particular task, issue, policy, crisis, or problem. The problems to be addressed by the participant may be either implicit or explicit, depending on the nature of the simulation.

- The subject matter, setting and issues inherent in the simulation are not textbook problems or questions in which answers are cut-and-dried and determined quickly.

- Participants carry out functions associated with their roles and the settings in which they find themselves.

- The outcomes of the simulation are not determined by chance or luck. Instead, participants experience consequences that follow from their own actions.

- Participants experience reality of function to the extent that they fulfill their roles conscientiously and in a professional manner, executing all the rights, privileges and responsibilities associated with the role. (p. 16)

The Teacher's Role(s)

We agree that education simulations typically have all of these characteristics. The complexity of simulations makes them powerful learning tools, but they also challenge teachers to design, conduct, and debrief them well.

Additionally, simulations require teachers to shed traditional roles, a stimulating, if sometimes unsettling, educational benefit. Lederman (1984) explained this role change:

> In the traditional classroom, the teacher's role is that of expert and the student's role is that of novice. The teacher is there to present; the student is there to learn from what is presented. . . . In the experienced-based classroom, however, teachers do not position themselves as experts, but rather as facilitators of learning; as helpers rather than leaders; as resource people rather than judges, evaluators, or testers. (p. 421)

In simulations, the teacher's responsibility—and power—to determine what and how learning will likely occur is modified by a shared power between teacher and students. Teachers must encourage learning by creating simulation experiences through which students will explore substantive content, develop discipline-specific skills, and apply what they know to real-world issues. Simulation teachers still assume responsibility for organizing the course, helping students understand the content and develop the skills necessary to pursue the inquiry, and evaluating students' contributions toward the shared goals as well as their individual learning. But the approach they take to fulfill these responsibilities will be far removed from the lecturer emoting behind a fixed podium.

Simulation instructors, above all, must become facilitators of the action. At the outset of the simulation the instructor explains how the simulation will work, what roles students will assume, and how to get the action started. Throughout the simulation, whether it covers only a part of a single class period or continues for several class periods, the instructor must decide how much—and how—to remain involved in actively guiding the simulation activities. We recommend that instructors lean toward giving students the autonomy to determine how the simulation will progress. This means at least sharing the leadership role of the class and in some simulation scenarios it may involve giving students the challenge and responsibility of guiding the progress of events. Many new simulation teachers anguish over the apparent risk in this, but in hindsight they universally consider it necessary to the success of the simulation. Each of us has our own level of comfort in this area, but the pay-off in student learning can be enormous if we can "let go." McKeachie (1994) reminded us: "The best answer to the question, 'What is the most effective method of teaching?' is that it depends on the goal, the student, the content, and the teacher. But the next best answer is, Students teaching other students" (p. 144).

Assuming the role of a character in the simulation scenario allows simulation instructors to retain some control of the activities. This type of involvement works for several reasons. First, the instructor retains a satisfying measure of control over student action without requiring students to move into and out of their scenario roles. The flow of the scenario action continues even as this guidance is taking place. Furthermore, instructors in a scenario role can guide students toward the desired learning objectives in a less obvious way, allowing students to benefit from the experience of framing and solving problems on their own. If you do assume a working role, select one that gives you the measure of control you seek without becoming the decision maker in the scenario. For example, if a learning objective of your course is a better understanding of the effect of discrimination in the workplace, you can design a relatively simple education simulation using the roles of (a) an employee who was—or was perceived to be—discriminated against, (b) the employee's supervisor, and (c) a common superior. Using this scenario, you could cast yourself as the company's human relations specialist, available not to make decisions, but to offer guidance to students playing each role. An even less controlling role might simply be to cast yourself as a friend to each of the students' roles.

As a simulation grows more complex or if you begin to use multiple scenarios in the same course (such as in the extended simulations we describe in chapter 7), we recommend that you assume a supervisory role. In such a role, you become involved only on an "as needed" basis to keep the activity moving without assuming a dictatorial role that might discourage students to risk making their own decisions. Examples of these supervisory roles in the Severely Concerned Inglewood Citizens (SCIC)/Inglewood scenario modeled in appendixes A and C might be the city council of Inglewood, the mayor of Los Angeles, or the administrator of the Federal Aviation Administration.

A final role that leads the instructor away from the podium is serving as the debriefer at the conclusion of the simulation. We have much more to say about debriefings in chapters 5 and 7, but we emphasize now that a well-orchestrated debriefing generates and reinforces much of the learning. The instructor must both design and facilitate this penultimate opportunity for learning.

Student Roles

The other people participating in education simulations are, of course, the students. Students, like instructors, also assume new roles in an education simulation. Lederman (1984) found that:

> [S]tudents do not take the same roles they are accustomed
> to in traditional classrooms either. They are not there as

> vessels to be filled—to listen and take notes and give the
> right answers to the questions teachers pose to test for
> attention and comprehension. Instead, they are there to
> engage in the simulation . . . to raise questions as well as
> formulate answers to questions regarding the connections
> between what has been experienced and what can be
> learned from that experience, to use their experiences to
> replace old cognitive maps with new ones . . . to think
> and to share what they think with their instructors. In the
> process of so doing, they hope to learn about themselves
> and the soundness of their own thinking. (p. 421)

Student participants in an education simulation are cast in functional roles as discipline-specific professionals and other characters involved in the scenario situation. Within the designer's rules
for the simulation, these participants are expected to assume these
roles and proceed as best they can to fulfill their real-world interests (recall the admonition not to "act" like a doctor, but to "be"
a doctor).

Students assume three types of roles in an education simulation. First are the essential or key roles, those central to the issue,
dispute, or conflict of the scenario. For most scenarios, these roles
are obvious. However, even after these essential roles are
assigned, you can modify them and modify the requisite activities
according to your learning objectives or depending on how students actually portray these roles, or both. Consider again our
example of a simulation scenario to teach various substantive
issues concerning discrimination in the workplace. If your learning objectives focus on (a) the effect such action has on individuals or the workplace or (b) the skills used to alleviate such discrimination, your essential roles would likely be, as indicated
earlier, the employee, the "offending" supervisor, and a management representative.

However, if your learning objectives focus on the legal aspects
of such a case (sufficiency of evidence of discrimination, due
process in handling complaints, or brief writing on the relevant
laws), you would design key roles to simulate the attorneys, medi-

ators, and judges necessary to the legal process. Similarly, if your learning objectives focus on the underlying government regulations, your essential roles might now be labor representatives, national business organizations, and government officials. And if understanding the economic costs of such discrimination was your learning objective, accountants, business leaders, and social scientists might be the essential roles your students would fill. You not only design the environment of a simulation to include real-life roles, but you also cast the essential roles in whatever way best achieves your learning objectives.

Students can also play a second type of role, one peripheral to the central action of the scenario. Characters in these necessary roles possess information important to the action and thus affect the decisions of students assuming essential roles. In any of these examples, the secondary roles might be coworkers, union representatives, others in the employee's supervisory chain, or interested outsiders to the main action, such as the media. Depending on the class size, instructors can use students to play these peripheral roles, or they may simply distribute "role cards" with written descriptions of these secondary characters, their interests, their knowledge, and perhaps "quotations" providing key information. Still other instructors assign multiple roles to each student so that they might play a peripheral role in a scenario within a simulation in addition to an essential role in a different scenario. This multiple assignment approach more closely approximates reality in that scenario, and it engages more students. We discuss this method of assigning multiple roles to students in chapter 7 when we explain our extended simulation. Examples of both essential and peripheral roles are demonstrated in the scenarios in appendixes A–C.

Students assume a third type of role by becoming simulation support characters. In these roles they represent a decision-making entity (a court, legislature, employee union, government agency, supervisor, etc.) to which students simulating an essential role may take the scenario action to further that role's perceived interests. The distinction of this role type is that the students may or may not become involved in the simulation action. For example, in the employment discrimination scenario the employee (or the employee's attorney or union representative) can be directed in the scenario to file an official complaint with the Equal Employment Opportunity Commission (EEOC). In this case the student simulating the EEOC would be filling an essential role. On the other hand, if the student filling the employee's role has discretion on how to deal with the issue—either total discretion or discretion within a limited number of options (options dealing with perhaps the work supervisor, a civil court, or the EEOC)—at least one student must be assigned and prepared to fill the EEOC role in the event that this body is consulted. Even if the role is not actually used in the simulation action, preparing for such roles can enhance the learning that occurs during the simulation debriefing by having students in these support roles discuss the effect their role *could* have had on the scenario. Such roles may be unnecessary or even distracting in a simple or short simulation; however, they are necessary for an extended simulation. We discuss these support roles more in chapter 7.

The information you give students about assigned roles remains critically important. This information includes background facts, instructions for critical tasks, and motivational reasons for taking an interest in the scenario action. Students should be allowed to bring their own personalities to the role, but their behavior must be consistent with the relative position of that character's role to the scenario and must further, and not impede, the learning objectives established at the outset. Chapter 3 discusses in depth designing a simulation scenario. In this overview, we highlight only a few key guidelines for creating the environment within which students will simulate their roles.

The Simulation Environment

The environment of an education simulation provides the context for the issues, problems, and conflicts students will face. This environment has little to do with the physical surroundings where the simulation activities take place. It deals instead with the situation into which student roles are placed to further their interests, the role descriptions, and the rules of conduct within which they must act. The context—the scenario—can be based on an actual situation or can be an entirely fictional simulation. It must, however, possess what Jones (1985) called "reality of function." This means that participants must be allowed to make their own decisions to further the interests of the roles they are assigned—as they perceive them. Thus, there should be no "canned" final solutions.

In the employment discrimination scenario presented earlier, the issue may be as simple as how an upset employee and offending supervisor can resolve tension in the workplace or as complex as having the employee pursue an unspecified legal recourse from among all that would be available in real life. The scenario directions may likewise be as simple as having two students simulate before the class a discussion between the employee and the supervisor or as complex as allowing for and supporting any real-world legal recourse with simulated decision-making forums.

The level of activities the instructor selects must be designed into the simulation scenarios from the start. Not everything should be spelled out in advance. For example, the rules for resolving issues are in part designed into the specific scenario story unfolding and in part established through the broader simulation management techniques discussed in chapter 4. Like a director of a stage play, the instructor's job is to create an environment that gives life to the roles and the means for the scenario characters to pursue their interests. Unlike most stage plays, however, the words and actions of the scenario characters are not scripted. Characters are allowed—and indeed encouraged—to "ad lib" within the simulation rules to further both their interests and the learning objectives.

The scenario of a simulation—a story involving specific roles and issues to be discussed, a problem to be solved, a conflict to be resolved, or a goal to be achieved—can also further creative "ad libbing." This involvement with learning goes far back in the educational record. The famous philosopher Rousseau noted: "One ought to demand nothing of children through obedience, . . . they can learn nothing of which they do not feel the real and present advantage in either pleasure or utility. . . . Present interest—that is the great mover, the only one which leads surely and far" (as cited in Finkel, 2000, p. 52).

The facts of the scenario can come from real life or they can be completely manufactured. However they are created, scenarios are presented to offer the issue, problem, conflict, or goal to participants in a manner that will induce them to take action to fulfill their "reality of function." Although they are abbreviated, modified, and accelerated, scenarios must seem real to the students. The parties involved, their interests, and their goals must be typical if not real, as must be their interests and goals. And the sequence of events in the classroom must flow in a true-to-life manner.

For the environment to appear true to life, the instructor provides students with information necessary both to determine their (role's) interests and to further them. The method of distributing this information can be accomplished in any of several ways, which we discuss in chapters 3, 4, and 7. The scenario story and the specific role instructions create interactions among participants. Additional information is presented in the form of documents, which can be anything that adds realism to the scenario: interoffice memoranda, letters, maps, government records, or new stories, real or fictionalized. As always, the two guiding factors are the instructor's learning objectives and the need for meaningful interactions—based on the "reality of function"—among students. For example, a simulation on "Labor Relations and Intergroup Conflict" (Mainiero and Tromley, 1989) clearly identifies three objectives related to labor negotiations, intergroup dynamics, and conflict. Furthermore, it clearly spells out instructions, a description of the P & M Manufacturing Company, bargaining issues, labor-management agreements among competitors in the New England area, and rules for negotiations. It is highly realistic.

Student interactions are the critical part of any education simulation. Thus, rules for facilitating and controlling these interactions must be carefully formulated. These rules might be as simple as deciding in what order participants are to act or as complex as developing decision-making bodies and their processes for students to use at their option. We save further discussion of these unique activities for chapters 3 and 5.

The final simulation activity, the debriefing, is the most important from a learning perspective. In fact, most educators believe that the real learning takes place during the debriefing. Occurring after the simulation activity, the debriefing goals clarify (a) what the student participants experienced, (b) what they learned, and (c) how they can apply that learning to future experiences and learning. Chapter 5 is devoted to this topic and chapter 7 contains suggestions for debriefing an extended simulation.

Think of people, environment, rules, and activities as the basic building blocks of an education simulation. As with physical structures, the more detailed and intricate the building materials, the more complex the structure becomes. We more fully describe these building blocks in the following chapters. We hope these first two chapters have at least given you a taste of education simulations and why you should consider using them in your course(s). If you like this taste, the next four chapters will give you a nourishing pot of soup—including how to design, manage, debrief, and assess education simulations. And if you like our soup, you will love the dessert in chapter 7.

3

DESIGNING AN EDUCATION SIMULATION

The first two chapters discussed what an education simulation is and some reasons why instructors might use them in higher education. Once instructors have made the decision to use simulations, they face three significant tasks: (a) designing the simulation, (b) managing its operation, and (c) debriefing and assessing it with the student participants. This chapter focuses on the first task, writing the scenario and developing the other necessary pieces of a simulation course. Chapter 4 looks at getting the simulation started and managing it, chapter 5 focuses on debriefing an education simulation, and chapter 6 emphasizes assessing it.

Ingredients Count Most

Because putting together a simulation does not follow a precise step-by-step approach, we caution against a formulaic platform such as merely using this chapter as a checklist. The simulations we have put together were actually made, as Jones (1987) said, like a good cook makes soup. Once you know what you are after, you have to gather the ingredients and begin to throw them into the pot. Some ingredients require no specified order. For much of the design phase, the creator, like an innovative cook, moves back and forth from learning objectives to role descriptions to tasks for students to adding pieces to the simulation environment. We suggest you do the same. Read this chapter not as the well-laid-out recipe in a gourmet cookbook but as something vaguely recalled from Grandma's description of creating a palatable education simulation.

Learning Objectives

A good starting point is to decide what your learning objectives will be for the course or the part of the course you will teach through a simulation. Your learning objectives are your guidelines. Start with whatever method you currently use to prepare for class. What topic are you teaching? Is it substantive knowledge, a skill, or a process? What do you want your students to take away from the course or this portion of it? What do you want them to remember or be able to apply 10 years down the academic road?

McKeachie (1994) and many other scholars emphasized the need to develop beforehand clear course objectives from which "all the decisions in course planning should derive" (p. 9). Such objectives, he exhorted, should:

> involve *educating students;* the objective of a course is not to cover a certain set of topics, but rather to facilitate student learning. Ordinarily we are not concerned simply with the learning of a set of facts, but rather with learning that can be applied and used in situations outside the course examinations. (p. 10)

Simulations are particularly adept at targeting a broad range of objectives that encourage the potential transfer of knowledge and skills into the workplace. Lederman (1992) recognized the broad learning objectives possible in a simulation: "The learning objectives are the specific cognitive, behavioral, and/or affective learning outcomes for the experience provided in the simulation activity " (p. 155).

Number of Students

In addition to the broadly based objectives, three key issues also affect the design of your simulation: (a) the number of students in your course, (b) the time you decide to allot to the simulation, and (c) the level of knowledge and experience of you and your students. Remember that the more simulation roles you design into your scenario, the longer it will take participants to complete their assigned tasks. To overcome the obstacle of a large class, you can have several groups of students engage in the same simulation at the same time. R. M. Narayanan (personal communication, October 6, 2001), an electrical engineering professor at the University of Nebraska at Lincoln, for example, has two to three teams of students work simultaneously on an actual request for proposal (RFP) for a radar-based project. Each team, headed by a project leader, is responsible for simulating the actual steps a corporate team would take to fulfill the RFP requirements. Adding an element of between-team competition, the final reports and professional presentations are evaluated by outside observers, including the RFP project manager, who determine which team is awarded the contract.

Another option is to assign several students to each role and have them work together. At the U.S. Air Force Academy, for example, in the capstone engineering course taken by all seniors, all the members of a class work simultaneously on a given project, usually a service-oriented one such as designing a swing for a handicapped child. Thus, it is essential that several students work together on a particular aspect of the project.

The first method usually provides for some valuable learning experiences during the simulation debriefing when different team actions and results are compared and discussed. Such approaches help develop critical thinking skills. Brookfield (1987) and others have emphasized that critical thinking depends on identifying and challenging assumptions and subsequently exploring and conceptualizing alternatives. The second method often works best when there is a wide range of experience, ability, and interest among students in a class. Simulations, being interactive experiences, depend on students giving it their full attention and effort. If teams of students are assigned to each role, there is a greater likelihood that someone in each team will participate enough for those students simulating other roles to gain the academic benefit of the simulation. Such team learning results in a win-win approach for everyone because of the value of peer coaching. Semb and Ellis (1994), for example, reviewed the research literature on the long-term retention of content taught in classrooms. They concluded that interactive classroom approaches, including peer tutoring, that "involve actively engaging learners in an enriched contextualized learning environment . . . should result in differential retention by making it easier for students to assimilate new information into existing memory structures or to create new well-organized ones" (p. 278).

Time

You must consider two critical aspects of time in an education simulation. First, think about the time it will take you to design the simulation. Even if you have participated in an education simulation before—which could be a significant benefit if it was designed well—plan to spend considerably more time preparing a simulation than you would spend preparing for a typical lecture or discussion class. Once you have designed a simulation, you can continue to refine it, but there is no substitute for the necessary up-front time investment.

Second, consider the class time involved. As emphasized earlier, three phases are involved in running a simulation: (a) the orientation of the students to the simulation, (b) the conduct of the simulation, and (c) its debriefing. Although we offer no magic formula for determining how much time to allot for each phase, experienced simulators find that the orientation and debriefing phases often add up to the time it takes to conduct the simulation itself. In longer simulations, this rule of thumb applies less because once students get started, they need less assistance. Also, students experienced with simulations in your class or another instructor's will need less time for the orientation and for the simulation itself.

Write About What You Know
Sources of Scenario Stories

Always keep in mind that, like a novel, you will write better if you write about what you know. One hopes that you are not in the situation of a cartoon character, Kudzu, who reflects on his knowledge base and begins to write confidently about the TV listings! You know the subject matter of your course. This knowledge will include the context into which you will place the subject matter, a context that will become your simulation scenario. Some scenario stories will jump out at you. They might be based on a personal experience. Or they might be based on a case study in the textbook you are using. If such flashes of inspiration occur, use them. You will be several steps ahead in the design process because you know the issues, the conflicts, and the characters. You may even have easy access to some of the relevant documents needed to flesh out the scenario. A biology text dealing with cloning, for example, is apt to include a current real-life issue. Whether you are teaching the process of cloning or its ethics, that example can be developed into a simulation scenario. For political or social scientists, the daily newspaper is filled with simulation scenario situations from local to international events. Students like the drama associated with a compelling story.

For example, V. Roettger (personal communication, October 29, 2001), an assistant professor of biology at Missouri Southern State College, enlivens her General Biology course by writing a crime scenario. She divides the students into three groups: the prosecution, the defense, and the jury. Within each group, the students decide who will be the lawyers, expert witnesses, the suspect, and so forth. They must then research the methods used for DNA evidence and present it to the jury. Will DNA analysis help determine the murderer? Resplendent in a black robe, Roettger presides over a classroom set up as though it were a courtroom. The "trial" lasts two days. Each side has a set time to make its case, question witnesses, and make final statements. They are allowed to use visual aids. The jury then deliberates and makes a decision, which the "judge" accepts. Afterward, each group writes a short paper—with references—describing what they researched and why. The papers are due a week after the "trial" concludes. The "jury," for example, writes a paper explaining how they came to their decision and includes the strong and weak points in the presentation of the defense and prosecution. They explain why one side presented a better case, made clearer explanations, and so forth.

Supporting documents used to add realism to the simulation include such things as the police report:

1. Twenty-three-year-old married female found dead in her apartment from a stab wound to the abdomen.
2. Time of death about 11 p.m.
3. Victim's brother and husband both live in the apartment.
4. Blood samples from the victim and scene were collected and stored for DNA analysis.
5. Neighbors heard yelling between victim and husband earlier in the evening.
6. Victim's parents died in an accident 2 months earlier and left a large estate to be equally divided between victim and brother who is currently unemployed.
7. Neither victim's brother or husband can account for their activities at the time of death.
8. Blood samples were collected from victim's brother and husband and stored for DNA analysis—both are considered suspects.
9. Later, the husband was arrested and placed on trial. (Roettger, 2001)

Herreid (1997/1998) made a compelling case for seeing stories even in the journal articles we write, specifically in science. He eloquently suggested:

> Each time we write an article for a journal we have a story to tell. Stilted and stylized though it may be, it is still a story. In the Introduction Section, we tell the children gathered around the campfire the reasons for the quest, the mountains to be climbed, the parchments we have read, and the dragons to be slayed. In the Methods Section, we describe the way we will tame the beasts of the forest, the preparations we have made, and the traps we have laid. In the Results Section, we tell of the happenings along our journeys, the magnificent delights we have witnessed, and the enchanted treasure we have discovered.
>
> Finally, in the Discussion Section, we explain to the king what it all means in the grand cosmic scene, why he should grant us his only precious child to take in matrimony, and why he should give us his kingdom in gratitude for the wisdom of the ages that we bring. (p. 6)

Looking at your discipline as a source of stories is a way not only to create simulations, but also to bring a powerful tool, the tool of storytelling, to the classroom.

Other scenarios you will have to create much like you would write a practical exercise problem or a fact pattern for an exam essay question. Even here, if you can find a similar case study to use as a guide, you will be well on your way. History simulations, for example, can draw on original documents such as field reports, particularly those that provide conflicting reports of a given battle such as the well-known Civil War engagement at Gettysburg. Many issues in a wide variety of disciplines are ready for use if they have been the subject of a legal battle, especially one that has wound its way through both the trial and appellate processes. The public records of these cases will provide the grist from which you can build a very exciting scenario. By contacting some of the litigants (best done after the legal process has concluded), you may acquire additional information and documents that are certain to add life to the simulation environment you are constructing. Another beneficial aspect of designing a scenario from a litigation case is that the key characters are already determined (which you can modify to suit your particular educational goals) as well as the issues, the controlling laws or regulations, and the affected parties. Yet another source for your scenarios are the news stories and reports in professional journals of your discipline. Often articles are prompted by a conflict of opinion or a newly discovered issue. Again, the core story and many of the core documents will have been prepared for you. You need only modify both to fit your learning objectives.

Reality of Function

Writing the scenario is fun. You simply write, or rewrite, a story about the situation as you want it simulated in class. Let the novelist emerge from all of your teacher training and experience. Keep in mind as you write your scenario story that you are creating a representation of the real world (and the real story on which your scenario is based). We come back to Jones's (1985) "reality of function" principle. Cunningham (1984) used the term "verisimilitude" when advising simulation designers to build a model that gives the appearance of reality and not to get either too realistic or too simplistic. He found, as we have, that education simulations "that are too realistic and complex may not permit the identification of the underlying learning objectives. . . . However, if a player finds that the simulated elements are too artificial, it may be viewed as simplistic and unreal" (p. 225).

Which aspects of the real world should simulation writers hone in on? Focus on those you want your students to learn about or those needed to create the reality of your scenario. Begin with just the basic facts and add to them only those elements that support your learning objectives or add fun to the simulation. Guard against adding so many facts to the scenario that participants feel that fact assimilation is the only goal. Central features of the model should be simplified, and less important elements should be jettisoned. Greenblat (1981) noted that a model becomes useful only if it highlights some elements and eliminates others (p. 43). Hopefully, reading the two scenarios at appendixes B and C will give you an idea of the issues we want our students to focus on as well as a feel for the interests of the essential roles we identified and the environment within which they must interact.

Avoid manipulating a simulation with your own personal message. The way you write the scenario will undoubtedly reveal some of your personal biases, but it is important to focus on the learning objectives you have established as your guide, not a personal agenda. Students quickly pick up on these extracurricular objectives and may reject the entire scenario/simulation if they feel they are being manipulated beyond the educational goals.

Scenario Characters

Two of the most important ingredients in your scenario soup are the character roles and the interests they will likely pursue. As indicated in chapter 2, three types of roles appear in most real-life scenarios. People playing essential roles act out the central scenario issue or conflict; people in supporting roles further the action of the scenario; and finally, people in secondary roles are usually affected by the outcome of the conflict, but do not directly affect it. For example, in a Russian history course, the leaders of the Bolshevik and Liberal parties would be essential players, the party members could play supporting roles, and the serfs could serve in peripheral roles. The actual situation will initially suggest what roles and how many should be built into the scenario. However, you do not need to represent every role. Select those key to the purpose of the action and important to your learning objectives. At the same time, you have the same license as a fiction writer to include whatever additional roles will contribute to the purpose of the simulation. If you have a few more students than roles, consider teaming them or assigning them slightly different roles representing the same interest (client and agent, project director and researcher, etc.). If you have significantly more students than roles, running simultaneous simulations is probably your best solution.

As you identify the roles of your simulation, begin to shape them in ways that best meet your learning objectives. If your scenario is built around a real event, begin to fashion the role descriptions after the actual participants. Change their backgrounds, their interests, and their goals as you see fit. Try to strike a balance between (a) giving students enough information about their role to allow them to identify their interests and to act professionally and (b) giving them so much that they need do little more than read the script you have prepared. Whatever character information you provide, encourage students to further develop the "personality" of their role consistent with the interests you have assigned to them.

Be certain to make the interests of each role clear to the assigned student. Impress on all of your students the need to act professionally within the context and the spirit of the scenario. In chapter 4 we discuss ways to ensure that the students assuming essential roles actually initiate the action so that things get going and so that students playing the other roles have something to respond to. Again, your learning objectives may shape the action within a narrow framework or they may allow maximum opportunity to interpret data, exercise initiatives, and resolve conflicts.

Secondary roles can be played out in several ways. The easiest is to simply write them into a scenario description, which you give to all students in the scenario. Examples of these roles might be marketing agents for new cloning research (if the learning objective is the ethics of the research, rather than how to make a profit from it) or witnesses to important events in the scenario. The students playing these roles would have to develop their characters from the scenario descriptions.

A second way to introduce these secondary roles is to assign a student to simulate a professional representing an essential role. For example, if a learning objective in a business management simulation depends on helping students understand how supervisors can deal with complaints of discrimination in the workplace, the worker and the offending supervisor arguably play essential roles. The offender's supervisor and an agent (lawyer, union representative, etc.) of the employee could be added as interested but secondary roles that would enhance the reality of the simulation and involve more students in the scenario. If you elect to do this, the background, interests, and actions of all the secondary roles must be considered and represented in some fashion in your scenario story.

The third and most direct way to include secondary roles in a simulation is to assign students to play them and provide these students with fairly complete character information. The students who play these roles will be available for students playing the essential roles to question and advise. You might select this use of secondary roles to promote secondary learning objectives such as gathering, interviewing, synthesizing, and analyzing information. Thus, you can give your students practice at these process skills while they are focusing on the main learning objectives of the simulation.

Support roles, the third type, are critical to an extended simulation, which we cover in chapter 7. People in supporting roles typically represent agencies and decision-making bodies that the students cast in the essential roles may engage to further their own interests. Examples are professionals from the courts, legislative or regulatory bodies, mediators, or anyone or any entity who has the power (in reality or in the simulation) to decide disputes, grant authority to act, or otherwise influence the action of the simulation scenario. In simple simulations without these varied options, such roles are unnecessary. If your learning objectives involve understanding skilled interactions with these bodies, the roles become essential rather than supporting.

Deciding what role you, as the instructor, should take is critical to your simulation. It is so important you should determine your role as you design the simulation. For certain, you must assume the role of the simulation administrator who explains what a simulation is, what it is about, how it is conducted, and when it stops. The real issue remains whether you take a role in the simulation scenario. Experienced simulation instructors argue strongly that the teacher should not assume a simulation role. Such direct participation can undermine, they suggest, the dramatic shift in a simulation from teaching to learning. Because students share the responsibility for their learning, they must take that responsibility seriously. For short simulations, we agree with this principle. Students must see and feel that they are in charge, that the decisions are theirs alone to make, and that they must assume accountability for those decisions. For most students, this sense of efficacy happens best and fastest if the instructor is completely removed from the simulation process.

However, an attractive alternative allows the instructor to assume the role of the principal for each of the roles the students are simulating. This instructor role fosters guidance for the "agents" in pursuit of their joint goals but still requires the students to determine the actual means to further those interests. Although assuming this supervisory role may appear tempting—especially after a simulation experience where students failed to perform satisfactorily in their assigned roles—we caution against it for short-duration simulations. You walk a difficult line between guiding student action and directing it. Additionally, the power of simulations lies not in having students identify the most effective "answer" or "goal," but instead lies in the learning experiences students engage in to find their own way.

In extended simulations such as the one we describe in chapter 7, we change this stance and encourage the instructor to assume the role of the simulation administrator and—only as needed—the principal to each of the roles assigned. We recommend these participatory roles because such simulations inevitably change directions, resulting in a need to keep students headed productively toward the learning objectives.

As you can see, selecting the roles you will assign to students inevitably proceeds simultaneously with the writing of the scenario. If you have a few more students than roles, you'll want to create a few more meaningful roles. If you want to add a teaching objective to your basic scenario, you will likely have to modify the scenario and add or delete students' roles. You are just adding extra ingredients to your soup.

Student (Role) Interactions

Once you have completed your scenario, you have to decide how to get the student interaction started. In most cases your learning objective will be more complex than merely having your students walk through the steps of a given process to accomplish what you have determined their interests and goals are. Afford them as much choice as your learning objectives and time allow. This approach is likely to mean they will make bad choices or even "fail" to accomplish their goals. This result is not necessarily bad. With your guidance, from these failures they will discover better ways to further their (role's) interests, and thereby learn. Be careful to keep what Loewenstein (1994) called a manageable "knowledge gap" for your students. If you make the gap between what students know and what they must learn too large, they will become frustrated as they attempt to fill in the chasm on their own. On the other hand, if this gap is too small, they will become bored because there is no challenge in accomplishing their tasks. "The enlightened individual is one who knows what he or she does not know, whereas a curious person is motivated to close the knowledge gap" (Burns and Gentry, 1998, p. 135).

At the design stage, you must determine whether your simulation will be closed (where you limit the options available to students) or open, and to what extent. A related issue is whether you will allow a student to make a choice that is the essential equivalent of quitting. You must decide whether to include any "impeding events," facts, or circumstances that make it difficult or impossible for students to complete their tasks. Whatever you decide on these issues, we offer two additional recommendations. First, do not get too "tricky" in your descriptions or taskings. Simulations are already hard enough and time consuming enough to eschew unnecessary distractions. Second, we recommend against having chance (the roll of a die, for example) determine the outcome of an action. As much as possible, allow student effort to have a direct impact.

Scenario Setting

Most scenarios require a setting, a place where the action is taking place. The most basic is the general geographic setting. The importance of this setting depends on its influence on the actions of the participants in your scenario. Conducting a simulation in the same geographic setting, such as Los Angeles, where your students reside has both pluses and minuses. On the one hand, you and your students will have easier access to documents, rules, organizations, and actual (or closely related) participants in the type of scenario being simulated. Students may even call on such real-life participants for advice. On the other hand, this proximity to real-life players can backfire. Some students, rather than determining on their own how they should further their role's interests, will seek the advice of real practitioners and merely act out what they are advised to do. Also, unless you develop a list of experts willing to make themselves available to your students, you run the risk of overwhelming these individuals with student requests for assistance and advice. Overtaxing these experts can strain relationships with the very people you may want to call on for assistance in the future.

The second setting of a scenario usually emerges clearly from the taskings to students. If they are asked to prepare a position paper to be used by a congressman, for example, the setting for its briefing becomes the House of Representatives. If they are asked to seek a change in the bylaws of a simulated corporation, the setting will be an annual or special meeting of corporate shareholders. You will not need elaborate props or scenery to bring this setting to life, but all participants must understand where the action of their scenario is to take place.

Before we leave the topic of writing a simulation scenario, we want to stress the importance of making the scenario interesting and fun. The "opening scene" should be written to catch participants' imagination and to get them to "buy in" to the scenario.

Scenario Documents

Somewhere in this design process you will have to add the spice—the documents that give flavor to the scenario soup. Some documents will be essential for the appropriate sense of reality. You can either obtain the real documents (and modify them as appropriate, which usually means simplifying them while still maintaining the "reality of function" we have previously discussed), or create reasonable facsimiles. These documents will consist of whatever would exist in the actual case being simulated—memoranda, maps, test results, newspaper articles, and so on. To whom you make these documents available, and when, goes hand in hand with how you wish to manage your simulation, another issue we discuss at length in the next chapter. Thus, as you are writing the scenario, you must consider the two most common options for distributing scenario documents.

The easiest way to distribute your documents is to give all of them to each participant at the outset of the simulation. They can then decide on their own—or you can tell them—whether each document is relevant to their interests, and if so, how. This method ensures that everyone gets the same accurate information. The major drawback to this method of distribution lies in its lack of reality. In life, rarely does everyone in any situation have the same information, or at least they do not obtain it at the same time. This fact leads to the second most common method of document and information dissemination.

In chapter 7 we discuss and give examples of what we call a selected and sequenced scenario. By this we mean that people playing selected roles in the simulation receive different information concerning their scenario background or role descriptions or that they receive different documents. Also, if you design a scenario that occurs in several phases (a design decision that critically depends on the time available in your course), this method allows students in selected roles to receive additional information as the action occurs—a more realistic situation. This is enough to say about this design feature now. As we mentioned before, just as designing a simulation scenario is a back-and-forth process, so too is the reading of this book. When we discuss this dissemination process in subsequent chapters, we are confident that you will be better able to understand our (and other authors') advice because we have mentioned it here. At the same time, after reading our later discussions, a rereading of this section will make a lot more sense.

Simulation Rules

The last two issues we cover in an education simulation design involve the rules you will use in your simulation. If your simulation includes decision-making bodies, such as courts, legislatures, boards of directors, agency heads, or organizations such as the National Science Foundation, either your students must be familiar with the rules of procedure for these bodies or you must include them in your instructions. If a focus of your course is on one of these bodies, you may elect to use its actual rules of procedure (adjusted to apply procedural time requirements to your class simulation). However, if your students are not at all familiar with the operation of such bodies, you should simplify their procedural rules to allow for their smooth and swift use in the simulation while maintaining a general sense of its processes. Remember that although unnecessary procedural details may be omitted, your simulation rules should not conflict with actual rules so significantly that they result in negative learning.

Rules controlling "student" actions during the simulation constitute the second type. We call these rules "instructions." How much freedom will participants have to act? May they act "illegally" or unethically? How are they to report their actions—in journals, written documents, or orally? How much time do they have to conduct their activities? Are there rules for the physical use of the classroom? When and how are they to contact each other and you? We agree with experienced teachers who have used education simulations that these rules must be manageable from the student's point of view. Unnecessary busy work and cumbersome activities should be designed out. At the same time, ease of administration is also an imperative. The more difficult a simulation is to administer, the greater the probability of distracting, if not devastating, administrative errors and lapse of control.

Remember, although a few more ingredients may add to the flavor of your soup, even at a very early stage in its cooking, it can be very nourishing. Serve it up: You can add those other ingredients as you discover a need for them.

4

MANAGING AN
EDUCATION SIMULATION

After you have selected or designed a well-constructed simulation scenario to use in your class, the chance of it accomplishing your learning objectives will depend on how well you manage the simulation. Some of this management will require you to make on-the-spot decisions to further your learning goals. However, most simulation management issues can be anticipated and planned for in advance. In this chapter we discuss many of these issues and offer suggestions for ensuring a well-run and rewarding simulation.

Management decisions determine the "flow" of the simulation activities, which significantly affects student motivation, participation, and learning. To provide this flow, you must carefully consider three key elements, all of them during the design stage. First, you must identify clear learning objectives. Second, you must design a simple structure that enables participants to move quickly and progressively through the planned activities. Third, you must provide appropriate instructions for participants about their assigned roles and how they will engage in the simulation activities. The longer and more complex your simulation, the more attention you must give to these instructions, which are distributed before and during the conduct of the simulation.

Preparing Participants

Orientating participants to the simulation experience is critically important. A productive orientation typically focuses on two factors: (a) the background, roles, tasks, and environment of the scenario; and (b) specific instructions for participating in the simulation.

Take time to familiarize participants with the scenario story and the key roles involved in the scenario. Explain enough facts to set the scene, to make the role descriptions and interests clear, and to allow participants to think professionally about their roles. Most scenarios will have a few essential roles requiring students to be responsible for initiating action or coordinating the action of several characters. Deliberately assign these roles to responsible students who are capable of these initiatives.

Duke and Greenblat (1981) identified several other factors to consider when introducing a simulation to participants, such as:

(1) Your early comments should include references to the following: (a) gaming-simulation as an instructional medium; (b) the purpose of the specific gaming-simulation you are employing that day; (c) the rules of the game in outline form; . . . (d) the roles represented by players in the room. . . . (2) Do not take too much time for the introduction. . . . (3) Sound decisive; if you convey the idea that you are sure it will be a good learning experience, you will be more convincing to players. . . . (4) Explain the expectability of initial confusion. . . . (5) Acknowledge that you, the game operator, recognize the nervousness and feelings of self-consciousness that some players feel. . . . (6) Sound enthusiastic. (p. 131)

Jones (1987) offered additional advice on what key points to cover in this initial briefing:

> If the students are unused to taking part in simulations, it is useful to spend some time explaining what they are and what they are not. The key points to emphasize are the extent of the powers, duties and responsibilities of the participants, and also the dividing line between reality within the simulation and the fictional background outside. Even if the students have taken part in simulations before, it is advisable to make sure they are aware of these points. (p. 80)

Assigning Tasks

The most important rule your students must adhere to during the simulation is to act professionally, always representing the interests of their roles. Stress that the point of the simulation is not to "acquire points" or to "win." Student learning and your assessment of their performance are based on their ability to apply what they have learned. This learning, which could have occurred in your class or in previous classes, will be used to accomplish assigned tasks that represent their simulated professional interests.

These tasks, based on learning objectives, are deliberately designed into the simulation. The tasks, which Parente (1995) called "deliverables" in his business simulation, may be either very specific (e.g., prepare a corporation's annual report) or general (e.g., prepare a new business development plan for a corporation). In both cases the tasks must be clear to participants. No matter how long you design the simulation to run, false starts will eat into the time allotted for your planned activities and adversely affect your learning objectives.

The assigned tasks are the heart of the simulation. They stimulate the action and provide opportunities for the application of knowledge and the development of skills. On another level they allow students to see the cause and effect of their decisions and actions. To avoid busy work, each task should be tied to a specific learning objective so that during a debriefing students can assess how well they have achieved that objective.

Maintain a separate list of tasks you assign to each student role. If the simulation requires students in some roles to take action or to respond to the actions of other roles, this task list enables you to ensure that the actions have actually occurred. Additionally, using this list as a place to annotate evaluations of student performances will assist you in your debriefing session and in assigning grades to students. We provide a sample of such a task list in appendix C.

Although we recommend that you assign specific tasks to accomplish learning objectives, you should nonetheless allow students maximum flexibility in how they achieve the tasks. Do not tell them how to behave. Jones (1985) advised that they "should be entitled to behave in whatever way seems appropriate in the circumstances, and with whatever powers, duties and responsibilities they would normally have in such a position" (p. 38). Does this mean they can lie, cheat, and steal? Again we agree with Jones that the answer is "yes"—so long as such conduct is within the realistic portrayal of the scenario role.

Distributing Information

You have two options for distributing information to the students about their role background and interests. The easiest way is to provide all of the information to everyone involved at the same time. This approach allows everyone to get the same picture of the scenario and provides the instructor with the most control. This method works particularly well for short scenarios where the key learning objective is to familiarize students with a discipline's substantive doctrine, skills, or processes. Appendix B is an example of this scenario type.

However, in most simulation scenarios—as in life—everyone involved in a scenario does not have the same information, and certainly not everyone is aware of the motives and interests of others involved in the situation. To better simulate this reality, you should prepare separate role descriptions and provide them only to those simulating that role.

To get the simulation action moving quickly, provide the students playing all roles with a general description of background events and the anticipated actions of the essential roles. Selectively distribute ancillary documents, background, and advice only to those students with roles likely to possess this information in real life. If your simulation scenario has several phases to it—and particularly if it extends over more than a single class period—distribute information and documents at appropriate times when the real-life characters being simulated would be likely to know the information. Appendix C is an example of this scenario type.

As we noted in chapter 3, your aim in designing a simulation scenario should be to establish and maintain a sense of reality. The documents you use should further this goal. "If they don't then you should ask yourself whether you are really trying to design a simulation or whether you are inventing a case study or an informal drama or a game or a teacher-controlled exercise or an accumulation of facts which require learning" (Jones, 1985, p. 37). The method of distributing these documents can enhance the sense of reality as well.

You can use varied means to distribute scenario documents and role information. You can prepare "hard copies" of role descriptions, tasks, and related documents, or you can store all of this information in electronic files for distribution by e-mail attachments at preselected times. If you use a course Web page for your simulation, you can store this information there and simply release selected portions of it to all or to certain designated participants at appropriate times. Once you begin to acquire a large volume of documents, it is easiest to maintain them in a single file, electronic or hard copy. Rather than actually distributing them to participants, you can then simply refer them to the appropriate file number to acquire it themselves.

Whichever method of document distribution you decide on, ensure that everything necessary for the simulation is available. Whether it is the first run of the simulation scenario or a subsequent one, check your materials "far enough in advance to obtain new ones in case any are missing" (Duke & Greenblat, 1981, p. 127). Again, Jones (1987) pointed out the special need for this preparation in an education simulation:

> The need for care in presenting the materials is not simply because it is more efficient to do it properly. Another reason is that in a simulation the penalties for mistakes are likely to be greater than in traditional teacher-student situations. . . . [I]n a simulation, which tends to develop a considerable dynamic quality of its own with a great deal of involvement, any delay caused by organizer inefficiency may well result in considerable exasperation from the participants. Furthermore, the mechanical breakdown may jerk the participants out of their roles, and it may take them some time to re-establish the flow and realism of the simulation. (p. 72)

In a simulation class, each role must be competently represented. Because both the action and learning of each participant depends on others, you cannot afford lack of participation. If you become concerned that a student working alone might be unable to fulfill an assigned role, consider assigning a group of students to simulate it. With the safety of numbers, you are less likely to have any role completely break down. Furthermore, students in a group simulating the same role benefit from discussing the role's interests and deciding on an action to take. By critically examining different options, they can more effectively evaluate them. Peer coaching also occurs, benefiting those who need the extra help but also benefiting those who are learning the material deeply enough to teach it to others.

Scenario Processes

As noted in chapter 3, processes involved in the simulated reality of your scenario should be simplified in the design stage as much as possible without creating an incorrect perception of the real-world process. Abbreviate the steps and simplify any forms or written requirements for the process.

The simulation environment evolves from the roles developed in the scenarios. The interactions of the roles, both directed by specific tasks and undertaken by the participants on their own, give further life to the environment. Do whatever you can to enhance the sense of reality of these interactions. For example, if possible, arrange for students in their professional roles to hold meetings in an actual conference room. At the very least, try to rearrange classroom furniture to appear like a conference room. Do the same if the action calls for a hearing or a trial before an adjudicative authority. Students simulating related roles should sit together to encourage familiarity and scenario actions. They should also dress appropriately for the role they are simulating, wearing, for example, business clothes for a formal hearing or board meeting. Establishing these standards of dress early in the simulation will set and maintain a professional atmosphere throughout the course (Parente, 1995).

If the simulation processes used by scenario roles are unfamiliar to students, prepare written instructions to guide them. If you anticipate a process will be used often during the simulation, consider asking one or more students to become familiar with the process and to be available to other students as advisers or assign them to roles directly involved in that process (e.g., as a court judge or legislative parliamentarian).

Instructions for Participants

Just as important to the flow of the simulation—and to student learning—are clear instructions for students aside from their scenario roles. Every administrative detail must be addressed, from class attendance to the format for written reports. Simulations depend on all participants doing their best to actively and professionally represent their assigned role. Accordingly, class attendance should be mandatory and participation should be weighted heavily in grading. Rules for student-to-student and student-to-instructor communication should be clear, especially

if the simulation is designed to run outside of class time. Requiring students to have access to e-mail and to check it on a daily
basis greatly facilitates communication.

Consider also the extent to which you will allow participants
to seek help from outsiders, such as actual practitioners of the
roles they are simulating. Some contact with these experts can be
very useful. However, as mentioned in chapter 3, student learning
will suffer if they merely execute these experts' recommendations.
Another consideration is goodwill; too great an imposition on the
time of these professionals will jeopardize their employment later
to the advantage of your course and your students. For extended
simulations, we offer several suggestions in chapter 7 on how to
gainfully employ such experts.

Instructor Management Role

Instructors should function as "facilitators" during the conduct of
an education simulation. This title "came into use not so much
because of its merits but because previous titles had failed to
describe accurately the activities of the person concerned" (Jones,
1988, p. 10). Simulations are not teaching events in the normal
context of an instructor-student relationship. In most cases, only
by removing the instructor from the direct action will students
fully assume their roles and take charge of the scenario action.
Jones's (1985) advice to instructors is to disengage yourself completely and quickly: "Disengagement on your part will convince
them that they are in charge, and that they do not need, nor will
they receive, your help and guidance" (p. 75). At first students
feel uncomfortable with this independence and, sensing their dis-
comfort, so will you. Resist your natural response to help. Even if
they accomplish fewer of the scenario tasks than they might have
with your direct assistance, students will assuredly learn more
working on their own. Most instructors have to learn how to let
the students run the class. As you observe student accomplish-
ments, this letting go will become easier.

Students typically seek assistance from the instructor in three
areas. First, they often want clarification on facts of the scenario.

Based on the importance of these facts to the meaningful progress of the simulation and to the learning objectives, the instructor may decide to (a) clarify the problem on the spot, (b) encourage the students to do the best they can to clarify the uncertainty on their own, or (c) guide them to helpful information.

Second, students often ask about the mechanics of the simulation, unrelated to the scenario facts. The guiding principle here is to keep the flow of the simulation moving. If the student's problem reveals a defect in the simulation design, correct it sufficiently to allow participants to continue toward the learning objectives. Because of the need to keep the flow of the simulation scenario moving, this area of student concern requires the most on-the-spot tinkering.

Third, students request advice on how to participate in their assigned role. There are two preferred ways to handle these questions. One is to inform students to make their own best evaluations of the situation and to take the action they feel best furthers the interests of the role they are simulating. The other is to act as a "senior partner" or "supervisor" to the role of the inquiring student and help them assess their position, interests, and options much as a professional supervisor would. If the student's decision seriously affects the action of students in other roles, offer sufficient guidance to keep the flow going.

Instructors should do everything they can to make the simulation easy to manage for themselves and easy to understand and participate in for students. Generally, these two goals are compatible (Elder, 1973) and what facilitates one aids the other. Students must be able to fulfill their role's tasks with minimum concern for the administrative requirements of the course. Reality of function for the roles requires students to "be" that doctor, not a student "playing" doctor. Managing—but not interfering with—the simulation is the best way to enable students to accomplish this transformation.

Creating and maintaining the proper atmosphere in your classroom during the simulation is as important as keeping the participants on task. The best advice is to keep all actions professional. Many participants get personally involved with their roles, to the point of being offended by the words or actions of others. Some students may even intentionally try to aggravate others in the belief that their negative behaviors may further the interests of their simulation role. In these instances, first determine whether such conduct is within or outside the students' realistic interpretation of the role and decide whether to approach these people as the characters they are simulating (you taking the role of their superior or some other person with simulated control over them) or as your students. Whichever tactic you decide on, do what is necessary to maintain a realistic and professional environment with a minimum effect on the flow of the simulation activities.

You are striving for a supportive environment. Apply the same principles during the simulation that will be evident during its debriefing. When commenting on the behavior of students in their simulation roles, describe their actions to them and discuss their effectiveness in accomplishing given goals. Avoid being directly critical of their personal behavior or beliefs. If a student is breaking an administrative instruction of the simulation, attempt to reorient them to the scenario purposes rather than directly telling them to take or to avoid taking a specific action. Accept unforeseen student decisions and actions so long as they do not destroy the learning objectives of the scenario. Some of these decisions will offer better "teaching moments" than you could have designed into the scenario. As necessary, stress to your students that the goal is to learn by doing, and that goal can be accomplished regardless of specific decisions or actions by any simulated character.

Managing Time

We shall end this discussion with one of the most limiting—and most influential—external factors affecting a simulation's design and flow: time.

In the design stage you had to consider several issues concerning time. How much time will students have to conduct the simulation during and outside of class periods? Will the simulation cover more than one class period? Will there be more than one distinct phase to the simulation and, if so, will the activity stop between phases? And, when in the course syllabus will the simulation be conducted? Such questions raise significant management issues as well, emphasizing our earlier suggestion that this book should be read "back and forth" between chapters to fully appreciate all of the components of designing and using an education simulation.

Where in your syllabus you should place your simulation will depend on such considerations as: (a) How much knowledge do your students need before they undertake a simulation applying that knowledge to simulated real-world facts? (b) Have students had sufficient time to acquire the specific discipline skills involved? (c) How experienced with simulations are the participants?

Regardless of the scenario you select or design, you must decide whether to conduct your classroom simulation within a scheduled class period or over more than one class period. Either way, we suggest spending some time before you begin acquainting your students with simulations in general and focusing on the specific one they will undertake. Jones (1985) prepared notes for his simulation participants that explained "what the simulation is all about, and what they can do and cannot do" (p. 35). You can do this at the beginning of class, during the preceding class, or in written instructions handed out to your students. Many simulations can be introduced (briefed), conducted, and debriefed in one class period. Students with previous simulation experience typically progress more rapidly and effectively through the various stages.

If you decide to run the simulation over several class periods, there are two typical ways to manage it. The first and easiest is to break up the simulation scenario into separate phases to fit into each assigned class period. Given the importance of debriefing (which we explore further in chapter 5), we recommend reviewing the simulation activities at the end of each phase. Whether you need to begin subsequent classes with additional orientations depends on the difficulty of the scenario and your students' past experiences.

The second way to manage a multiclass simulation involves providing participants with instructions at the outset and allowing the simulation activities to occur at the participants' choosing. Chapter 7 provides a detailed explanation of a version of this type of a complex simulation, which we call an "extended" simulation. The extended simulation we describe is designed to run an entire semester. Whether your simulation runs that long or not, chapter 7 will help you understand and evaluate additional management considerations beyond those for a simple one-class-period simulation.

To provide a better representation of reality, simulations can accelerate normal time periods or create deadlines that align simulated processes with the class schedule. This timeline is relatively simple if the scenario calls for specific and identified activities, such as preparing a plan of action or actually simulating a specific action, such as filing an employment discrimination complaint with the EEOC. However, the more a freedom a scenario gives participants to determine what action they will take, the more consideration the designer must give to the relationship between real time and simulation time. "Insofar as possible, deadlines should flow logically from the sequence of activities or events being simulated" (Elder, 1973, p. 345).

If a simulation covers an unspecified period, during which participants engage in precisely sequenced activities, the scenario designer and manager must ensure that each student role is operating on the same relative simulated timeline. Remember in the design process to crosscheck the tasks of each role to match times and deadlines. During the actual conduct of the simulation, keep a list of all planned actions and match them to the class syllabus. In chapter 7, where we describe our extended simulation, we offer additional advice on how to manage this real-time/simulated-time issue.

Designing and managing an education simulation to *save* time is another important "time" issue. Eliminate real-world process steps that impede or do not support learning objectives. Allow students to submit written tasks in whatever format they choose or in a simple, straightforward format you design for them (unless, of course, the form or format is important to the course's learning objective). If your simulation involves more than one step for participants, give a specific time limit or deadline for each step to keep the activities flowing according to your predetermined timeline. In a multiple-step simulation, allow time between steps for quick feedback and reorientation of participants toward the next objective.

With all of the activities going on in an education simulation and all of the learning objectives planned to be accomplished, guard against your simulation being "rushed and pushed into some fixed time slot, leaving a feeling of dissatisfaction among all concerned" (Jones, 1988, p. 75). From your initial orientation to the conduct of the simulation to the debriefing, be sure you allot *enough* time.

If your simulation is managed well, not only are you more likely to stay on your schedule and accomplish more learning tasks, but you will have set the stage well for the final phase of a simulation: the debriefing.

5

DEBRIEFING AN
EDUCATION SIMULATION

In the last chapter we explored the skills an instructor using simulations must develop to manage the conduct of an education simulation and discussed how they differ from the teaching skills required in a traditional classroom. Similarly, instructors must use different assessment methods to measure the extent to which students have achieved the course's learning objectives. In a traditional classroom, teachers commonly lecture; the linear communication is focused on the teacher; the students take notes; and the learning is determined by the amount and accuracy of the information transferred to the student, as measured by a content-based test. In an education simulation, teachers facilitate activities among students; communication is interactive, nonlinear, and student focused; and the measure of effectiveness is determined by the knowledge, skills, and abilities the students take away from their simulation experiences. The assessment of this learning takes place not during a terminal content-based final examination, but during the simulation debriefing (Lederman, 1984).

The Debriefing Process

Debriefing is "a process in which people who have had an experience are led through a purposive discussion of that experience" (Lederman, 1992, p. 146). Used for centuries by the military, debriefings helped settle soldiers after often traumatic military engagements or focused missions while helping commanders develop new strategies for future engagements. We hope that education simulations will not prove traumatic for participants, but they should definitely be focused. Debriefings can, however, disengage students from sometimes emotional activities, settling them down and helping them become more receptive to meaningful discussions of their simulation experiences. According to Crookall, editor of *Simulation & Gaming* (1992), "The debriefing objective will indeed be twofold—not only to help the participants learn, but also to help them resettle after what can sometimes be a stressful event" (p. 141). The business world has also long used "postpresentational sessions or postmeeting analysis," and as the military connotations waned, a debriefing "was viewed as the means for sorting out afterward what had happened during the experience; simply stated, it was a recollection of that experience for the purpose of learning from it" (Lederman, 1984, p. 416).

During the debriefing of an education simulation, students transfer what they have experienced into meaningful learning where—under the guidance of the teacher—they "replace old cognitive maps with new ones" (Lederman, 1984, p. 421). During the debriefing, students relate their experiences to the substance of the course's content, discipline-specific processes, and skills. They should also "learn about themselves and the soundness of their own thinking" (Lederman, 1984, p. 421). Through this reflection on the simulation experience and a guided analysis of what occurred, students can integrate the experience into their life as a basis for future learning and experiences, thus increasing the likelihood of transfer of knowledge and skills in an actual professional setting. "A key finding in the learning and transfer literature is that organizing information into a conceptual framework allows for greater 'transfer': that is, it allows the student to apply what was learned in new situations and to learn related information more quickly" (Bransford, Brown, & Cocking, 2000, p. 17). Thatcher (1990) agreed that debriefing is the most important part of an education simulation, declaring it a "process by which the experience of the game/simulation is examined, discussed, and turned into learning" (p. 270). Thiagi (Thiagarajan, 1992) agreed that debriefing "is an instructional process that is used after a game, simulation, roleplay, or some other experiential activity for helping participants reflect on their earlier experiences to derive meaningful insights" (p. 161).

In this chapter we discuss specific reasons (besides the principal one of learning) for conducting a debriefing of an education simulation. We focus on three distinct phases of debriefings, offer suggestions from several teacher-authors on how to conduct it, and present lists of questions used by experienced simulation instructors to facilitate this critical part of an education simulation.

Depending on the scenario used, students may not be aware of all of the events that took place. Even if all students were present throughout the simulation, however, it is doubtful that everyone had the same experiences. Students brought different backgrounds to the simulation that influenced their perception of it and affected its direct effect on them. Thus, a debriefing is necessary to help all participants recall the key experiences of the simulation, and, as important, as Palmer (1998) noted, to seek the "community of truth." He carefully described these complexities:

> As we try to understand the subject in the community of truth, we enter into complex patterns of communication—sharing observations and interpretations, correcting and complementing each other, torn by conflict in this moment and joined by consensus in the next. The community of truth, far from being linear and static and hierarchical, is circular, interactive, and dynamic. (p. 103)

A solid debriefing also allows those who were not direct participants in a simulation event to learn from it.

Lederman (1984) cautioned: "Knowledge that is the product of experience is highly subjective" (p. 417). Instructors must ensure that students acquire appropriate knowledge and skills. The debriefing is also important to correct errors in student analysis and performance. Because students often bring misconceptions to a given subject that may remain uncorrected, Bransford et al. (2000) encouraged faculty members to "strive to make students' thinking visible and find ways to help them reconceptualize faulty conceptions" (p. 71). Students can give too much credibility to a simulation experience, whether that experience was an accurate reflection of real-world events or not. Instructors must guard against this "negative learning." The most effective moment for this correction is immediately after the error. However, the instructor may not be aware of every decision or activity or be in several places at once where different actions of the simulation are playing out. Sometimes the instructor may intentionally let a mistake occur to create a better "teaching moment" to discuss during the debriefing.

Planning a Debriefing

Debriefings of a simulation experience require careful planning and execution to achieve the greatest learning. They can assume a variety of formats: oral or written, individual or group, immediate or delayed, or any combination of these. Most debriefings are conducted as guided discussions, the most common and efficient method. The discussion method works particularly well because, as Thatcher (1990) noted, the "process of articulating one's thinking is a vital part of the process of converting experience into learning" (p. 266). In fact, Brookfield and Preskill (1999) identified 15 benefits of a well-conducted discussion (pp. 22–23). They advocated using the discussion method because "at its best, discussion greatly expands our horizons and exposes us to whole new worlds of thought and imagining. It improves our thinking, sharpens our awareness, increases our sensitivity, and heightens our appreciation for ambiguity and complexity" (p. 20).

If the group of participants is small enough, it is best to have everyone participate in the discussion. If the group is large, the time set aside for debriefing is short, or both, you may have to select another option. One possibility is to open the class up to voluntary discussion rather than insisting on participation from all. If you decide on this approach, try your best to keep a few talkative students from dominating the discussion. Another option is to request those students playing essential roles to discuss their experiences while you build on their comments to emphasize your learning objectives. Still another way is to have a small group of students in representative roles engage in the debriefing while others observe (this is Steinwach's, 1992, "fishbowl" method). This approach is an obvious choice where a team of students was assigned to simulate a single role, but it can prove valuable even if participants each play separate roles, so long as those who played essential roles participate in the debriefing group. The debriefing group arranged in a circle discusses the simulation experiences while other classmates stand behind their chairs, taking notes and essentially evaluating the content and process. In some fishbowl scenarios, the standing participants can join the inner circle when they have something important to contribute, typically by tapping the shoulder of seated debriefers and taking their places. A final option for large groups is to divide them into smaller groups to be debriefed separately. This requires the instructor to repeat the debriefing several times, or it requires additional personnel (and space) to conduct simultaneous debriefings, assuming suitable debriefers are available.

Regardless of the format you select, debriefings typically occur in several phases. However, before we discuss these phases and how to conduct them, we offer some considerations you should give to planning a meaningful debriefing.

During your design of the simulation, develop a detailed plan for the debriefing session(s). First determine how much time you will need. Although there is no formula for the amount of time needed to debrief a simulation, initially plan on at least 25% of the time scheduled for the entire simulation. If your simulation runs for several class periods, this overall percentage may decrease. However, several factors will also increase the time required for a meaningful debriefing: a large number of participants, a lack of student familiarity with debriefing, and a large number of phases or activities in the simulation action.

No matter how much time you allow for debriefing, plan to change the physical layout of your classroom for this activity. If you have the space, arrange students on chairs in a circle. This rearrangement quickly and dramatically puts students into different relationships than they shared during the conduct of the scenario activities. A circle also places them visibly in the same relative position to each other. In addition to changing the physical arrangement of the classroom, try to create an atmosphere that differs from the simulation setting, one that is nonthreatening and supportive. Compliment the group and let them know that their decisions during the simulation will focus the debriefing with a positive emphasis on lessons learned and ways to improve decisions in the future. Be affirming of everyone who speaks. Lowman (1984) emphasized that teachers should indicate that they, too, are participating. The atmosphere should promote mutual inquiry, not mere recitation with "students showing off what they know or that they have done the reading" (p. 133).

The same learning objectives that molded your simulation scenarios will allow you to structure your debriefing and prepare in advance how it will be conducted. Prepare questions to prompt student discussion based on anticipated or actual simulation activities. We have several generic—but helpful—questions already selected, which we discuss later. The task list you created in the design phase to help you track activities while you were managing the simulation action will aid you considerably in preparing additional questions for the debriefing phase, particularly if you made comments during the action.

Many simulation instructors also require participants to submit some type of written reflection on their experience as well. This makes sense because, as Leamnson (1999) reminded us, encouraging and facilitating student thinking remains central to learning and "the real evidence for thought, clearly, is language" (p. 24). In a multiphase simulation, consider requiring this written reflection after each of the activities, much like journals. If the simulation takes place over several days or class periods, journals provide a wonderful way to capture individual reflection, analysis, and feedback. Fulwiler (1987) recommended using journals "actively every day to write in, read from, and talk about—in addition to whatever private writing the students do on their own" (p. 15). He found that their active use makes it difficult for students to hide passively.

Regardless of its frequency, written reflections help students integrate their simulation experience with their prior knowledge and experiences and force them to organize their thoughts and emotions, enabling their more productive participation in a group discussion. Instructors require these written reflections for many reasons: to capture details of what happened and student rationales for them, to allow students to share any emotions engendered by the simulation, and to give students an opportunity to note personal issues or questions that they might not mention in a group setting.

Written reflections also allow for more comments than an oral exchange and provide an opportunity for a private exchange of student thoughts. And they provide instructors with valuable resources to use in assessing/grading each student's participation and performance.

To save time, consider giving students a format for written comments that parallels how you will conduct the oral debriefing. We outline a useful method for conducting a debriefing next.

Conducting a Debriefing

Plan and conduct the debriefing as a clearly distinct part of your simulation. Do whatever you can to separate the simulation scenario activities from the debriefing. Have students turn in any materials you want returned. If the debriefing will occur during the same class period as the scenario action, at least take a short break. If you changed how students addressed you during the simulation, switch back to your normal teacher title. Have students sit in different places or in a different arrangement, such as the circle we suggested. A circle suggests equality among students and because the teacher is not set apart, it also implies a regard for student opinions. It usually encourages active participation. However, Brookfield (2002) also cautioned that students can't hide in a circle: They "know that their lack of preparation, or their poorly articulated contribution, will be all the more evident to their peers" (p. 265). Because a circle configuration can be tortuous for painfully shy students, you should consider explaining the rationale for this set-up.

Similarly, it is important to explain to all of the participants how the debriefing will be conducted. If you decide to have distinct phases to discuss certain topics, let students know. If you want to hold to firm time limits, set them in advance and keep to them. Let students know at the outset of the debriefing whether you have firm or flexible rules on who can speak, about what, or for how long. If you have required written reflections on the simulation activities, allow students a few moments to review their comments before engaging them in the debriefing. Some debriefers establish specific ground rules. Brookfield and Preskill (1999), for example, used these six:

1. No one may be interrupted while speaking.

2. No one may speak out of turn in the circle.

3. Each person is allowed only three minutes to speak.

4. Each person must begin by paraphrasing the comments of the previous discussant.

5. Each person, in all comments, must strive to show how his or her remarks relate to the comments of the previous discussant.

6. After each discussant has had a turn to speak, the floor is opened for general reactions, and the previous ground rules are no longer in force. (p. 81)

Your debriefing should address three aspects of your students' participation: as people, as the roles they simulated, and as students. This balance recognizes both the complexity of the simulation and the human elements involved. Students have brought to the simulation their unique background knowledge, experiences, personalities, prejudices, and expectations. No two individuals bring the same things. Each is also likely to react differently to the scenario, their role, and other participants. Allow this individuality to come through in each person's comments, especially their initial ones.

Depending on the simulation and the people involved, emotions can run high. On a personal level, elicit what participants feel about their experience. Are they satisfied with the experience? Are they upset, angry, embarrassed, or elated? Give them some time to gather their thoughts about their feelings. If nobody volunteers, try to get the discussion moving by mentioning student comments from previous simulations. Try your best to understand why each person feels the way he or she does. Be supportive, not judgmental. Just listen to and accept what the students say. Not all strong feelings need to be aired, especially if conflicts exist among some of the students or between some of them and you. You will never get to the heart of the learning if your students are upset and are thus unwilling to contribute. Lowman (1984) emphasized that "the classroom is a highly emotional interpersonal arena. . . . All students are vulnerable to such disrupting emotions, and some students are especially sensitive to them. Also, like anyone else, students have a potential to react emotionally when they are being challenged and evaluated in group settings" (p. 12).

Several experienced simulation administrators begin this part of the debriefing with the simple question "How do you feel?" Lowman (1984) commented that "including qualifying terms such as 'what you know,' 'what stands out,' or 'mean to you,' emphasizes that it is students' personal thoughts the teacher is interested in, not their ability to produce a 'correct' answer" (p. 132). Discuss how a given student's personal behavior may have affected the interests of the role they were simulating. Do what you can to encourage them to delve deeper into their explanation or analysis of their role in the scenario. Do not use this time to lecture them about the subject of the scenario and do not tell students what they should have learned; the goal is to get them to uncover their own learning. Try your best not to get defensive over criticisms of the scenario or the instructions or the way the simulation was conducted. It is very important that you affirm each person's statements and get everyone to participate. If emotions run high during this early phase of the debriefing, take another break before transitioning to the more analytical phases.

Cultural or political considerations can raise the emotional level of a simulation, including the debriefing. For example, Staley (private conversation, December 18, 2001), a professor of communications at the University of Colorado at Colorado Springs, remembers emotions running extremely high during a simulation called "Power Lab" (Mainiero & Tromley, 1989). She divided a class composed of adult students in the former Soviet Republic of Kazakhstan into three groups: a top group, a middle group, and a bottom group. Directed to construct rectangular buildings, the top group held all the money and virtually all the power. By the end of the simulation, the bottom group was ready to rebel, the middle group was thoroughly frustrated, and the top group remained ever arrogant.

The next phase of the debriefing focuses on the roles assigned to participants and the roles' interests in the scenario(s) that the students were asked to promote. Although you do not want the debriefing to be a continuation of the scenario action, allow all participants to describe their interpretation of their role's interests, motivations, and decisions leading up to the actions taken during the simulation. First, guide them through a description of what happened during the simulation. Even if everyone received the same information, each role had different interests that were likely to shade that person's perception of the simulation activities. And if you elected to give different or selective information to different roles, participants will have to listen to others to get the whole story. This should take the form of a recap of events, allowing every role to describe what they did. This discussion should result in several "aha" moments among the participants as they acquire a new understanding of the simulation activities. It will also encourage each person's self-reflective processing of his or her own experiences.

Encourage students to candidly reveal to the other participants what information they had, what tasks they were trying to accomplish, and what their plan was. Ensure that everyone remains clear about which role each student played. You may elect to have participants fully describe their character's role activity in the simulation one at a time. However, we recommend a guided discussion of all roles involved in a scenario as the action occurred. This way each participant can explain an action and others can comment on how they perceived that action, what options it generated, and why they responded the way they did. This discussion should unfold in a logical format that closely follows the students' combined experiences. After all participants—or at least those involved in essential roles—reveal these insights, you can guide a meaningful discussion of the simulation focusing on the overall learning objectives. Encourage students to reveal their thoughts on the rationales and actions of other participants, keeping their comments focused on the scenario roles rather than on personal attacks.

You are seeking insights into the meaning of the experience to your students. They will often perceive facts and even interpret assigned tasks differently from what you intended. This does not mean they were wrong: Be careful not to suggest this. At the very least, they are providing good feedback to help you improve the scenario directions for your next class. Be empathetic rather than judgmental of the students' explanations. Build on this discussion to guide students toward your learning objectives, which is the focus of the next stage of the debriefing.

If you designed the simulation scenario with the appropriate "reality of function," the debriefing of simulation events will lend itself to an expanded discussion of real-life parallel events. Come prepared to point out these analogies but try first to draw them out of the students with leading questions. Learning "sticks" in this phase of the debriefing and forms a new foundation on which future experiences and knowledge can rest.

During this phase, debrief all of the participants as students. Cover the simulation action in terms of learning objectives, emphasizing other course material leading up to the simulation. Draw on prior learning and discuss how the knowledge and skills obtained during the simulation can be used to enhance future learning. Be mindful and attentive that this phase of the debriefing does not wander off into tangents far removed from your learning objectives.

Use this occasion to address substantive issues in your course or related courses and texts. Tie the course's doctrinal, organizing principles to the practical applications experienced in the simulation. Relate specific scenario tasks to the course's learning objectives. Analyze why things happened the way they did. Reinforce the appropriate things learned and, sometimes more important, correct the mistakes or improper assumptions made during the simulation. Depending on the time and discussion progression, discuss what students could have done differently—insert some "what if" questions—and reflect on what differences those alternative actions would likely have made. Most important, link simulation experiences to past learning and events, and to facilitate transfer, help students make connections to future learning and experiences, particularly in the professional world.

Debriefing Questions

Several educators and authors of articles on education simulations stress the importance of developing questions in advance that can be used to prompt student participation during the debriefing. (Lederman, 1992, 1984; Thiagarajan, 1992). We have added some of our own and tied them to the different phases of the debriefing portion of an educational simulation.

Dealing with emotions:

1. How do you feel?

2. How did you feel when _____ did _____?

3. Did your feelings change during the simulation?

Describing simulation action:

1. What happened? How did the action unfold?
2. What was the scenario about?
3. What was the major interest of your role?
4. What did you do?

Personalizing the action:

1. Why did you take a certain action?
2. How did (another role's action) cause you to (re)act?
3. What were the implications (of your action)?
4. What were your greatest successes and frustrations?
5. What were your greatest obstacles; how did you overcome them?
6. What would you do differently next time? Why?

Apply the simulation to past and future learning:

1. What were the key issues?
2. How did the scenario relate to the typical issues of the course discipline?
3. What did you learn?
4. How was the experience worthwhile?
5. What would have occurred if other decisions had been made?
6. What would you do differently next time? Why?

Applying the simulation to the real world:

1. How does the simulation compare with real-world behaviors? Give examples.
2. Was it predictable? Why?
3. What real-life issues were missing in the scenario? What effect did this have?

Good questioning can produce genuine learning:

> Isadore Rabbi, a Nobel-prize winning physicist, tells a story of when he was growing up in the Jewish ghetto of

New York. When the children came home from school, their mothers would ask them, "What did you learn in school today?" But Isadore's mother would ask him, "What good questions did you ask today?" Dr. Rabbi suggests he became a physicist and won the Nobel Prize because he was valued more for the questions he was asking than the answers he was giving" (Costa & O'Leary, 1992).

Simulations may not lead to Nobel prizes, but they can significantly increase student learning and motivation.

6

RESPONSIBLE ASSESSMENT

When teachers identify their least favorite aspect of the job, most of them answer, "Grading." This should be no surprise: Probably no aspect of teaching has a greater impact on student learning than the grading system. Grades have enormous consequences. They affect students' motivation to learn, their perceptions about the teacher's integrity, and their relationships with one another. Lowman (1984) called grades "an unpleasant and unavoidable reality" for both teachers and students (p. 185). Pollio and Humphreys (1990) stated:

> Grades, grading, and the uses made of them strongly affect the academic climate within which teaching and learning take place. With the exception of very few institutions, grades and the grading game are the basic facts of academic life for professors and students, and they influence in many and varied ways important interactions between teachers and learners. (p. 109)

Grading pressure may be aggravated, ironically, by simulation classrooms where the instructor assumes a benign, supportive role but still maintains the power to determine an athlete's eligibility to play football, a scholarship student's financial status, or a would-be medical student's class ranking. Furthermore, unless clearly spelled out from the get-go—a practice we strongly recommend—grades in a nontraditional classroom can be a source of anxiety and potential conflict. McKeachie (1994) reminded us:

> The student's anxieties about grades are likely to rise if their instructor's procedures make them uncertain about what they must do in order to attain a good grade. For many students, democratic methods seem unorganized and ambiguous. In any ordinary course students know they can pass by reading assignments and studying lecture notes, but in a student-centered class they are in a course where the instructor doesn't lecture, doesn't make assignments, and doesn't even say which student comments are right or wrong. The student simply doesn't know what the instructor is trying to do. Thus, if your teaching and grading procedures differ from those your students are used to, you need to be especially careful to specify the procedures and criteria used in grading. (p. 112)

Grading students, which is only one aspect of assessment, may include features such as student self-evaluations and peer critiquing. Additionally, because of the complexity of simulation courses, savvy instructors also offer opportunities for formative assessments, ways that both teachers and students can determine what and how well students are learning. In fact, Bransford, Brown, and Cocking (2000) recommended designing classroom environments that further these critical assessment aims:

> Formative assessments—ongoing assessments designed to make students' thinking visible to both teachers and students—are essential. They permit the teacher to grasp the students' preconceptions, understand where the stu-

dents are in the "developmental corridor" from informal to formal thinking, and design instruction accordingly. In the assessment-centered classroom environment, formative assessments help both teachers and students monitor progress. (p. 24)

Furthermore, assessment of the course or aspects of the course—particularly the simulation scenarios—will help instructors more skillfully design, execute, and debrief future simulations.

Grading, thus, is a complex process that, at its best, can produce positive results. Walvoord and Anderson (1998) took an enlightened view of grading:

Grading, then, includes tailoring the test or assignment to the learning goals of the course, establishing criteria and standards, helping students acquire the skills and knowledge they need, assessing student learning over time, shaping student motivation, feeding back results so students can learn from their mistakes, communicating about students' learning to the students and to other audiences, and using results to plan future teaching methods. When we talk about grading, we have student learning most in mind. (p. 1)

These positive learning goals, however, can be undercut by the system of grading you employ. Simulation courses should involve noncompetitive grading practices: Students pitted against one another have no reason to cooperate to enhance the learning—and hence the higher achievement—of fellow students.

Noncompetitive Grading Practices

Grading on the curve, most experts agree, is detrimental to student learning (McKeachie, 1994; Nilson, 1998; Walvoord & Anderson, 1998). It basically establishes a quota system. As indicated earlier, simulations can be particularly effective in capstone courses and preprofessional courses. The caliber of students enrolled will be high because they have made it that far through the system, and they have chosen to specialize. Thus, it seems unethical for instructors to announce at the beginning of the term, "Only the top X percent of you will earn A grades. Those in the next X percent will receive B's, and so forth." Such quotas kill any incentive for students to support one another's efforts. Because students are negatively interdependent (one student's success means that another student cannot be as successful), they have no reason to help one another's learning, thus undercutting the cooperative philosophy needed for simulation teaching. Additionally, grading on the curve can have other negative effects. Students may feel isolated and excluded, or they may feel helpless because their individual efforts are not directly connected with their course achievement.

Rather than grading on the curve, we recommend that teachers set up a valid criterion-referenced grading system based on student achievement. All students who reach a specified level of competency earn the desired and appropriate grade. Nilson (1998) stated that criterion-referenced grading "requires instructors to set absolute standards of performance (grading criteria) in advance, giving all students responsibility for their own grades" (p. 196). Such a system thus promotes diagnosis and mastery. Part of the design process will include specifying the assessment criteria, which should encourage motivation that is both extrinsic (effort based on the reward of positive grades) and intrinsic (learning for the sake of learning). In support of extrinsic motivators, Chance (1992) pointed out that "reinforcement is probably the most powerful tool available to teachers, and extrinsic rewards are powerful reinforcers" (p. 121). Kohn (1993) urged teachers to use intrinsic motivators. He advocates "an engaging curriculum that is connected to . . . [students'] lives and interests. For an approach to pedagogy in which students are given real choices about their studies and for classrooms in which they are allowed and helped to work with one another" (p. 124).

In higher education, grades are often the primary extrinsic motivators. No teacher who has heard the dreaded words, "Will this be on the exam?" can doubt their power. However, the research on intrinsic versus extrinsic rewards is clear in higher education, as we saw in the literature on deep learning. "An anxiety-provoking assessment system that rewards or tolerates regurgitation of factual material—material students are not intrinsically motivated to learn—promotes shallow surface learning" ("Deep Learning, Surface Learning," 1993, p. 1). On the other hand, a mastery orientation toward learning can promote positive motivation. Students need a sense of control over the final outcome. They should feel they have responsibility for their own grades and can take positive steps to improve them.

The literature on effective student evaluation is voluminous. Constructing a clear, fair, and functional evaluation system is challenging. However, you have a good starting point: Just as your learning objectives shape the scenario you select or design to use for your simulation course, they will also determine your assessment mechanisms. For example, Astin et al. (1992) noted:

> Assessment is a goal-oriented process. It entails comparing educational performance with educational purposes and expectations—these derived from the institution's mission, from faculty intentions in program and course design, and from knowledge of students' own goals. . . . Clear, shared, implementable goals are the cornerstone for assessment that is focused and useful. (p. 2)

It is important, also, to aim for embedded assessment, assessment practices that amplify the learning without being merely "add-ons." For a course intended to transfer knowledge and build professional skills, you might require written papers and oral presentations from students. To incorporate such work into the context of the simulation scenario, these assignments can take the form of a briefing paper to a managing board, a business proposal, or draft legislation. Each of these assignments (simulation tasks) can be assessed and graded in the same manner you would any other student assignment. If your course learning objectives focus more on discipline-specific formats for writing—case summaries, economic analyses, and the like—simply design these into the simulation and grade them as you normally would.

Simulations, as group activities, also lend themselves to assessment of how well each student worked with others. Although subjective in many respects, such performance can be observed and assessed. Advise students at the beginning of the course that you will be observing and grading their decisions and actions throughout the simulation as well as their ability to work with and influence other students in their group. The following are a few of the criteria you may identify for grading student performance:

1. Demonstrated understanding of substantive issues.

2. Understanding and proper use of processes.

3. Representation of role interests.

4. Demonstrated initiative.

5. Quality of written work.

6. Quality of oral presentations.

7. Demonstrated ability to work with others.

8. Demonstrated leadership.

9. Effective time management.

The sheet describing the interests and assigned tasks of each role is a convenient place to make contemporaneous notations about student performance. These notes can help you manage the simulation activities. It is helpful, also, to keep these notes on student performance for later use in making recommendations to potential employers. You will be able to discuss your students' abilities far more meaningfully than instructors who base an opinion only on students' answers to questions in class and on their performance on written exams. Employers familiar with your course and your grading policies (especially former students) will seek your recommendations. Keep these performance notes for all students in your simulations, along with the roles and key tasks they fulfilled. Thus, an awareness of student participation, whether it is graded directly or not, is essential.

Evaluating Students' Participation—or Not

Student participation is often a significant portion of the grading rubric in a simulation course. An advantage of a discipline-specific simulation is that each student will have specific tasks to accomplish and identifiable interests to promote during the activities. Assessment can then be based not only on this activity, but also on how much and in what manner students advanced their role's interests. Innovation and persistence can be rewarded as much as results.

Having said that, it is also fair to say that grading students individually for their participation during group activities is problematical at best. Jacobs and Chase (1992) identified some of the inherent difficulties: Instructors rarely spell out the criteria for evaluating the value of the participation; they don't coach students on how to improve their participation scores; shy or introverted students are often disadvantaged; record keeping can be a daunting task; participation scores, which might be considered too subjective, are open to challenge. Furthermore, with simulations, an instructor cannot be involved with all groups at all times. In fact, few faculty can accurately monitor the behavior of more than two students at once. Therefore, students should not be assessed for their group contributions for each in-class activity. You can either consider your simulation activities "business as usual" and not assign participation points, or you can use peer and self-assessments to help you determine a fair grade. Too often the teacher is thought to be the only one capable of providing viable assessment. In reality, however, when independent work and group work are involved, peer and self-assessment become even more meaningful than the teacher's insights. Furthermore, Speck (1998) felt that student peer and self-assessment are needed to resolve the ethical dilemma of an instructor in two essentially conflicting roles, that of coach and that of evaluator: "Is it fair for professors to be both coach and judge when they don't seem to be able to defend their dual role outside of an appeal to professional status" (p. 26)?

Peer Assessment

There are many justifications for peer assessment even though students, unless properly trained and similarly committed to the practice, may be hesitant about passing judgment on their peers. Allowing student input into the process of evaluation sends several signals consistent with the "community"-centered course environment needed for successful simulations:

1. Teachers, because they are not the sole arbitrators of success or failure, play less of a gatekeeper role responsible for weeding out the unfit and the unworthy. The process of evaluation is shared.

2. Students are in a logical position to be able to judge, far more effectively than an instructor, the individual contributions of their peers.

3. Peer feedback in a simulation is usually directed toward an individual within the context of a specific task. Thus, besides being context specific, it tends to be delivered promptly when feedback is most effective.

4. Peer evaluation builds in accountability: Students realize they are held accountable for their academic achievements and group contributions. They may be able to "psyche out" a teacher, but they can rarely hide from their peers.

5. Students benefit from the process of peer review. They learn valuable skills about the learning process and about teamwork efforts.

6. In the process of evaluating one another's performance, they are also acquiring powerful professional skills needed in the workplace when they will need to evaluate those they supervise.

Because of accountability and equity issues, teachers should monitor carefully any peer review process. Students must be assessing peers on attainable course objectives based on carefully specified criteria. They must offer concrete evidence. Woods

(1996) advocated training students to do such assessments and providing an environment where peers can give accurate feedback. He suggested:

> Create an environment that rewards fair and accurate assessment. We can do this by making assessment a learning objective for the course. That is, students are assessed on their ability to assess others. . . . The peer assessment is never considered to be "Let's say nice things to our friends." Rather it is a skill under development. (p. 5-9).

Peer assessment can become more meaningful when students have input and ownership over the process. For example, in business courses where performance appraisal is a topic of study, students can develop their own criteria for evaluation and create instruments to use for overall peer assessment or for selected tasks or segments in the simulation. Hobson (1998) reminded us that "using student-generated criteria—whole or in part—requires professors to concede that students can articulate what distinguishes strong performance" (p. 54). Peer review is obviously complex. Woods (1994) integrated peer review into virtually every aspect of his problem-based learning engineering classes. Feedback, whether given by himself or by peers, typically addresses five strengths for every two things that could be worked on. After all group meetings, students complete a feedback form that looks at both their task performance and their group skills.

Student Self-Assessment

Researchers involved in determining how to promote deep learning have focused their attention on students actually engaged in learning by observing, listening, and probing as students study in specific contexts. As Rhem (1995) concluded, "In the end, they have focused on metacognition as the heart of learning and view it as a phenomenon more influenced by the demands of particular learning environments than by predispositions of personality" (p. 2). Similarly, Bransford et al. (2000) considered metacognition essential to learning. With a solid research base and clear implications for teaching, they conclude that "a 'metacognitive' approach to instruction can help students learn to take control of their own learning by defining learning goals and monitoring their progress in achieving them" (p. 18).

This recognition of the role metacognition plays in learning makes it desirable for teachers to include self-assessment opportunities in courses. Woods (1994) placed self-assessment at the heart of learning. Students should learn to evaluate:

- the subject knowledge,

- the problem solving skills used,

- the group process used,

- the chairperson skills displayed,

- the acquisition of self-directed, interdependent, lifetime learning. (p. 8-3)

With assessment comes accountability for both students and teachers. Assessments must be conducted responsibly based on measurable criteria, evidence, and objectivity. Woods noted: "Self-assessment is one of the most powerful educational tools available. Being challenged to set personal learning goals motivates and focuses our energies. Having skills in the assessment process puts us at an enviable advantage for life" (p. 8-5).

Classroom Assessment Techniques

Related to self-assessment because they also give students insights into their own learning, classroom assessment techniques (CATs; Angelo & Cross, 1993) provide instructors with a systematic, student-centered way to find out if and how well students are learning. By using the focused, formative feedback provided by CATs, faculty can make midcourse adjustments in their teaching to help students learn better. CATs give instructors a particularly useful way to ascertain the effectiveness of unusual teaching methods, such as simulation learning.

CATs offer students and faculty at least three key benefits. First of all, because students are actively involved in the CAT activities and receive feedback on their responses, instructors are helping students develop the metacognitive skills crucial to learning. CATs make the process visible. Bransford et al. (2000) concluded:

> Because metacognition often takes the form of an internal dialogue, many students may be unaware of its importance unless the processes are explicitly emphasized by teachers. An emphasis on metacognition needs to accompany instruction in each of the disciplines, because the type of monitoring required will vary. (p. 21)

Second, because these embedded techniques encourage faculty to vary their teaching approaches in responsible ways, students often enjoy these classes more than traditional classes predicated on one-dimensional techniques such as lecturing or even guided discussion. As the old cliché has it, "Variety is the spice of life!" As Duffy and Jones (1995) pointed out, instructors must work to stimulate and motivate students, particularly during the interim weeks of a semester where it may become necessary to beat the doldrums. And third, teachers receive richer personal rewards by turning teaching into a dynamic and intellectually stimulating activity in its own right. They begin practicing in a systematic, proactive way the scholarship of teaching advocated by Boyer (1990) and others.

In conclusion, faculty report, according to Angelo and Cross (1993), these "four observable, interrelated, positive effects of Classroom Assessment on their students: more active involvement and participation; greater interest in learning, self-awareness as learners, and metacognitive skill; higher levels of cooperation within the classroom 'learning community'; and greater student satisfaction" (p. 372).

For a full range of CATs, we recommend that you consult Angelo and Cross (1993) or chapter 12 in Millis and Cottell (1998). We discuss in this chapter only three CATs that are particularly suited for simulation teaching and learning.

Background Knowledge Probe

According to Angelo and Cross (1993, pp. 121–125), by sampling students' level of preparation, the background knowledge probe (BKP) helps teachers determine the most effective starting point for their lessons. This feature of the BKP also makes it particularly valuable to simulation facilitators because they can identify students most suited to handle the demands of essential roles.

The BKP consists of a short questionnaire administered before a simulation, whether it is a short one-class-period simulation or an extended simulation as described in chapter 7. By evaluating these responses, teachers garner an idea of the knowledge and experiences students bring to the class at the outset. Teachers should carefully develop the BKP questions with this objective in mind. Before initiating the BKP, instructors should identify the knowledge, skills, and abilities they would like ideal students to bring to the simulation. Often, we assume students hold knowledge they do not possess, especially about a topic familiar to us. If we falsely assume certain background competencies, we may fail to provide the coaching or background information students need to successfully complete the tasks required in the simulation, overwhelming them with seemingly unrelated information that they cannot connect to prior knowledge.

A well-designed BKP will contain a range of questions ascertaining students' preconceptions and misconceptions, subject-related knowledge, and attitudes and potential motivation. As with all CATs, BKPs are formative rather than evaluative. You should therefore design and administer CATs so that students do not feel as though they are taking a test.

Having collected individual responses on the BKP, the instructor evaluates the student answers and divides them into groups. Angelo and Cross (1993) suggested four piles for BKPs: [−1] erroneous background knowledge, [0] no relevant background knowledge, [+1] some relevant background knowledge, and [+2] significant background knowledge. With this helpful information, you can more confidently assign students to simulation roles. You will also know what informational gaps need to be filled in before beginning.

As an example, if a nursing instructor were to begin a simulation that involved interviewing patients who might be at risk for AIDS, a BKP might include questions that probe for (a) students' preconceptions/misconceptions about AIDS, (b) knowledge about the North American Nursing Diagnoses (NANDA) List of Approved Nursing Diagnoses, (c) students' factual knowledge about AIDS, and (d) students' knowledge of basic interview skills in the nursing profession.

Pro and Con Grid

Simulations invariably contain content areas where a particular course of action has benefits and drawbacks. Thus, students' understanding of a topic may depend on their awareness of more than one side of an issue. As virtually every student development model suggests, this awareness is a difficult but valuable step in students' intellectual development. The pro and con grid (Angelo & Cross, 1993, pp. 168–171) provides important information on the depth and breadth of the students' analysis and their capacity for objectivity.

With simulations, student team leaders playing essential leadership roles will use these grids. We recommend adding a third column to the grid, "caveats," after explaining to students the meaning of that term. Thus, a simulation pro/con/caveat grid would look like this:

Preferred Decision	Pros	Cons	Caveats

To use this CAT, you should encourage the students assuming key leadership roles that involve a decision, a judgment, a dilemma, or an issue to consider involving others in the decision by using this systematic approach. Before calling a meeting, they can distribute the grid and ask each participant to complete it, giving, if desirable, a specified number of pros and cons, with attendant caveats. For example, a simulation might involve a management decision with conflicting mandates of (a) improving the quality of care in a financially ailing hospital, (b) maintaining credibility—with political funding ramifications—of helping the needy in the community through off-site clinics, and (c) setting the financial house in order. Using prepared pro/con/caveat grids, students playing various roles could debate the various options and come up with the most viable solution(s).

Self-Diagnostic Learning Logs

Simulation instructors may view self-diagnostic learning logs (Angelo & Cross, 1993, pp. 311–315) as limited, tightly focused versions of academic journals. You can use them only for the simulation portion of your course, or you can ask students to complete them on an ongoing basis during an extended simulation, a practice recommended by Angelo and Cross (1993) and explained in greater detail in chapter 7. Students need to know that the purpose of their learning log is to enhance their ability to learn course concepts and principles and to help them become reflective, self-directed learners. On a prescribed day, students hand in a one-page learning log report that answers questions such as the following: (a) Which course concepts or principles were useful to you in working the current problem or issue? Where did you learn them?—from independent research? from the textbook? from other students? from the simulation coach? from outside experts? (b) Which course concept or principle that you previously learned did this new concept or principle build on? (c) If you experienced difficulty or were unable to work the problem or issue, what information or knowledge would have enhanced your ability to work it? Where could you have obtained this knowledge?

Students writing learning logs are forced to identify and communicate the course concepts they are applying. They therefore learn these concepts and principles to a much fuller extent than by simply focusing on the solution. We also recommend, as with the pro/con/caveat grid, having students discuss their responses with other students to expand and reinforce learning.

Learning logs also give instructors added insights. By reviewing them, you can identify aspects of the simulation that confuse students and can respond with carefully focused instruction. Moreover, the learning logs cause students to practice and improve their writing skills, particularly in quantitative disciplines, thus enhancing their marketability in a world that relies more and more heavily on rapid and effective communication. As should be obvious, none of these CATs should be divorced from an overall assessment of the simulation experience.

Assessment of the Simulation

A recent Ziggy cartoon portrays a diner asking the waiter if the fish is fresh. Despite an obviously poisoned customer lying face down on a table to the waiter's back, the waiter confidently replies, "We've had no complaints." Teachers, like waiters, cannot be oblivious to what is actually going on. Thus, assessment of all aspects of the simulation, including activities, learning, student-student interactions, evaluation procedures, comfort levels, and so on, are essential. During the debriefing of each simulation, you should build in time to solicit opinions from the participants on how the simulation could be improved. At the very least, ask participants to identify what did and did not work during the simulation and to offer their suggestions to improve it.

An efficient, although relatively impersonal, means to obtain feedback is with a questionnaire. Questionnaires, if well designed, have the advantage of allowing data to be efficiently quantified, particularly over time. However, the data may be difficult to enter, depending on resources, and they may be difficult to interpret, depending on the appropriateness of the questions.

Many simulation instructors welcome the benefit of having a colleague visit the class to offer insights and advice. Well-conducted, collegial observations can be powerful tools for constructive changes (Millis, 1992). Successful classroom observations should accomplish at least two goals. They should reinforce positive behaviors (things the instructor is doing right), and they should lead to changes in behaviors to strengthen teaching (things the instructor could improve). Thus, a skilled observer will both offer information and provide inspiration. Based on the observation, the simulation instructor should know what to change and be motivated to make the changes.

Another assessment alternative is to conduct 1-hour focus groups with the students. We recommend a protocol developed at the U.S. Air Force Academy. Unlike traditional focus groups relying solely on open-ended questions, the protocol uses two structured activities to capture data that can be quantified and effectively displayed through Excel charts and color-coded Word tables. To evaluate a simulation, depending on the size of your class, you would use the protocol either with the entire class or with a representative sample. Twelve is an optimal number.

As the students arrive for the focus group, the facilitator (typically NOT the simulation instructor) gives each of them a brief survey with idiosyncratic questions such as these using Likert scales: (a) "How much time did you devote to simulation preparations?" (b) "How much time do you estimate your classmates devoted to simulation preparations?" (c) "Please indicate your comfort level in the class." The survey could also included open-ended questions such as: (a) "Briefly describe your most positive experience during the simulation." (b) "Briefly describe an experience that you would not wish to repeat. Please explain why." After discussing the purpose of the focus group and ground rules, such as listening attentively and providing respective responses, the facilitator tells the students the session will be audiotaped. To ensure confidentiality, the facilitator instructs each student to use a number they acquire through a count-off, rather than their names. Students quickly adopt the practice of saying things such as: "This is Number 8. I agree with Number 5's comment about a few slackers slowing down our progress, but I think that Number 12's conclusion is correct: The simulation overall was a fantastic learning experience."

In the first structured activity, students receive an index card. Working independently, they jot down on the card a word or phrase to describe the simulation experience and a number from 1 to 5 indicating their satisfaction with the simulation. Usually the facilitator has the students indicate, round-robin fashion, their responses. These data are later displayed in an Excel spreadsheet with the height of the columns dictated by the number of people giving the simulation a specific number. Within the columns are the words or phrases they used.

At the conclusion of the index-card activity, the facilitator then asks about four open-ended questions using PowerPoint slides as prompts. These questions have been carefully selected by the simulation instructor to extract key information, particularly information that would be embellished by the synergy of a focus group discussion. The instructor also decides which questions all students should answer and which are suitable for random responses. Typical questions for a simulation focus group might be: "What were your expectations for this course? Were they met?" "Did your experiences with the simulation help your learning? In what ways?" "Describe the working relationships of the students portraying the various simulation roles."

After these questions, the facilitator then moves to the heart of the focus group protocol featuring a structured activity that enables students to identify and clarify their own issues. The facilitator places the students into groups of 3–5 students, giving each group a handout with specific instructions to brainstorm all the strengths of the simulation and then to brainstorm all the things about the simulation that could be improved. These two activities follow rapidly, one after the other, so the students don't get into an analytical mode. Called a roundtable, the paper circulates rapidly from one student to another as each adds an idea, saying it aloud. After these two roundtables, each group then rank orders the strengths of the simulation and then the weaknesses. The rank-ordering activity is critical because it enables students to reach consensus on their priorities and to eliminate any idiosyncratic responses. The roundtables and the ranking together take only 10 minutes of the 60 minutes available. The data can be presented in a series of lists for each group or they can be placed in a Word table where common elements from each group are color coded. For example, if all four subgroups rank ordered the equivalent of "Helps our understanding" as a strength of a simulation, that strand might be color coded in yellow, enabling the simulation instructor to easily recognize the consensus among groups.

After the roundtable/ranking activity, the facilitator typically asks more open-ended questions for a total of 8–10 questions. All the audiotaped questions can then be transcribed so that a full record of the comments, including the debates among students, is available for review. At the Air Force Academy, the audiotapes are transcribed by a medical transcription service, but a talented secretary could also produce the script. If clerical support is an issue, taping is unnecessary if a second facilitator captures the gist of the conversations on a laptop computer.

In addition to gathering data from questionnaires, classroom observers, or focus groups, your own self-reflection—either on the data or simply on the simulation experience itself—is critically important. Soon after the simulation is completed, take time to review how it transpired and modify role descriptions, remove ambiguities from assigned tasks, obtain or revise necessary documents, and consider meaningful debriefing comments. Just as designing an original simulation course involves a great deal of working back and forth among its various pieces (scenarios, role descriptions, taskings, management tools, and assessment mechanisms), the best simulations are those that are continually modified from use to use. That is why multiple forms of assessment and responsible feedback become an essential part of a simulation-based classroom. Assessment should never be considered an "add-on." It is an essential part of the learning process and, like it or not, an essential part of faculty work.

AN EXTENDED
SIMULATION

What Makes a Simulation "Extended"?

Relatively simple educational simulations can take from several minutes to a complete class period. Others naturally carry over to a subsequent class period by simply allowing students more time to carry out their objectives or by staging different phases of the education simulation experience during successive classes. Once you do this, you begin the journey down the road to what we now describe—an extended simulation. There is no magical moment or length of time when an education simulation becomes extended, and we define one as any simulation that continues beyond a single event or phase. The example we describe here, however, is a semester-long course using a single simulation containing several overlapping scenarios.

Before attempting this type of simulation, you will need more planning and more management tools than are required with a simple simulation. However, we are convinced that once you try one, you will become hooked on this exciting method of teaching and learning.

An extended simulation is designed and used for the same reasons less complex simulations are—but for many more reasons as well. Rather than meeting a single or only a few learning objectives, an extended simulation may deal with dozens of learning objectives. Every aspect of a simple simulation is expanded. Not only are there more learning objectives, but the objectives also overlap in ways that force students to discover—working independently or working in groups—how best to achieve them. Additionally, these objectives can be placed in a more realistic context within your discipline. The roles that students assume come to life in an extended simulation with greater opportunities to develop. Not only will students deal with multiple issues affecting the interests of the roles they are simulating, but also as they "become" these roles, they will discover interests beyond those you designed into the simulation. Simulated public and private organizations will also take shape, exerting their own influence on the scenario activities. Abbreviated but real-life processes will become familiar to students as they use them to solve assigned problems. Relationships between roles will form in ways the *students* will decide. Your classroom will be transformed into a completely new environment ripe for learning.

All of this will happen because you will have added the one critical element missing from limited educational simulations: more time. Additional time allows students to develop their assigned roles; to determine on their own what their interests are within the scenarios in which you place them; and to test their understanding of the substantive material of your course against more realistic situations than those provided by textbooks, exams, or even simple simulations. As with other simulations, students will apply their knowledge and skills. In addition, they will have to find and interpret the processes, regulations, and policies of practitioners of your discipline to further their assigned interests in professional ways.

No magic formula determines when all of this happens, but it always does, and it is indeed magic when it occurs. Students begin to think, act, and talk, not like students, but like the people they are simulating. Additional time allows them to work through the processes of your discipline, observe others working through them, and deal with the results of those processes, perhaps even working through them again. An extended simulation not only calls on participants to use their prior experiences, but it is itself a significant experience from which participants will learn and on which they will build future knowledge and experiences—some to be applied later in the simulation.

Time allows students an opportunity to assess the best interests of the roles they are simulating, act on that assessment, observe the reaction of others involved, challenge others or be challenged for the action they elect, have that challenge resolved, and react to that resolution. With proper feedback, this simulation action takes case study and problem-solving classroom activities to another level.

Time, the critical element, allows the educational environment you design to take its real form. Although some props will prove beneficial, the personification of the characters causes the transformation. If you have ever been to a stage play with minimal scenery—perhaps just spotlights on different areas of the stage to represent different scenes—and yet been amazed afterward about how "real" the play seemed, you know what we are talking about. The reality comes from the sincerity of the actors in their roles and their interactions in the drama (your well-created scenarios). The luxury of time in an extended simulation allows these wonderful manifestations.

Just as in a great play, additional time alone will not bring out the best in your extended simulation. You—the "playwright"—have to select the right ingredients to make this play—or "soup" if you stay with Jones's metaphor—your Tony Award winner. In this chapter, we offer directions for selecting your story, for creating your plot and your conflicts, for staging them in a realistic way, for managing the actions, and for debriefing an extended simulation to achieve your learning objectives.

We describe how to select, design, and present scenarios to be used in an extended simulation and how to develop them into usable tools. We discuss how to create and assign multiple roles for students. And we describe the special environment needed for an extended simulation course. For an extended simulation to work properly, you must blend real-world characters, events, and environments with the simulated ones you create. The information in this final chapter should at least whet your appetite for a simulation soup if you are an adventurous instructor and provide the last measure of encouragement needed to get you started on what will assuredly be one of your most exciting experiences in teaching.

The comprehensive extended simulation method described here does not consist simply of a series of vignettes set up, played out, and analyzed. Here, you assign the roles of practitioners actually involved in discipline-specific real-world activities at the start of the course, with your students playing them throughout the semester—in class and out—before the same (simulated) forums the actual practitioners do. The various skills and processes of your discipline will mold the shape the action of your extended simulation scenarios. Instead of a single scenario with limited roles, you begin with multiple scenarios, each involving several roles. The more you extend a simulation, the more you will begin to see roles overlap. A governmental body, a commercial activity, or a private entity will become involved in several different scenarios at the same time. If there are no obvious or natural overlaps, you should craft some. Modify scenario facts just enough to make a governmental agency the same one that deals with roles in several scenarios. Involve the same commercial enterprise in various activities of your scenarios. Assign a role—a homeowner's association, businessman, politician, and so on—similar interests that are involved in several of your scenarios.

Although extended simulation teaching can accommodate fewer students, we recommend at least 20 so you can create the complexity of interactions necessary to bring your simulated world to life and give your students the best educational experience possible. Also, although this pedagogical approach can work successfully in introductory courses, we recommend its use for higher level electives within a discipline or for capstone courses. In this type of course, students continually apply substantive knowledge, taking them to deeper and broader understandings of their discipline.

The extended simulation method we describe was originally designed for teaching law students, but the principles are applicable to any preprofessional course, including engineering, medicine, business and management, psychology, and so on. Many of the examples we offer are thus framed by our original goals of teaching students to "think and act like lawyers," but you will want to establish your own discipline-specific goals. With our example, to accomplish this overarching goal required a program of education and training that took students well beyond being able to brief a case or research an issue. Lawyers—those who get paid by clients—have to achieve client-centered goals. These goals focus thinking and action. If the law is against these goals, lawyers seek new legislation. If the legislature is also against them, lawyers negotiate or seek alternative political solutions. If the client's interests are harmed or threatened, lawyers sue. There is never only one alternative. Identifying a client's goals and deciding how best to achieve them are what "thinking and acting like a lawyer" is all about.

Additionally, even in our law school setting, many students assumed nonlawyer roles, those necessary to create the desired environment and to play the many important roles that would further the learning objectives. We found that casting law students in these other roles heightened their awareness of the varied interests other parties invested in issues, and it gave them greater insights into the issues themselves. We are confident that this approach is just as applicable to other disciplines—accounting, business, health care, political science, sociology, management, and so on. If there is a limit, it is only the instructor's imagination. The method can be adapted to almost any purpose.

This method of teaching also allows—in fact, it practically requires—you to bring several features of your discipline together for your students. In a single extended simulation scenario, for

example, you can require students to research doctrinal principles, write a persuasive position paper, deal with private and public opposition, negotiate a solution to a controversial problem,
and withstand a challenge to the ethicacy of their action. In cooperation with instructors from other disciplines, you can design an
extended simulation course that crosses traditional academic
boundaries and explores the applications of more than one discipline to real-world issues.

Extended simulation courses challenge students to solve
selected problems through innovative approaches. They encourage
your students to consider influences and consequences beyond
those you present. You need not be an expert in any of these other
areas, but you should be experienced enough to recognize the
issues and to discuss them in general terms. We offer suggestions
on why and how to obtain assistance with unfamiliar areas.

In a simulation course of this magnitude, you must create a
complete environment within which to support both the real
world and the academic problems built into the course. Students
can tackle problems using real-world approaches, yet the simulation structure allows additional academic control and experimentation. Students' knowledge and abilities are tested against your
planned academic challenges, but they will also encounter
unplanned challenges from their classmates playing other roles.
Continuous developments, adjustments, and breakthroughs,
planned and unplanned, are vital parts of this academic learning
mode. By allowing students significant control over the activities
in the simulation, you provide them with a greater sense of
responsibility for their actions, and they become freer to test the
limits of substantive theory and practice as well as their own
capabilities.

During an extended simulation, not only will students have
opportunities to apply knowledge and skills to real-life issues, but
instructors will also have greater opportunities to observe student
performance, both in terms of time and variety of learning situations. These opportunities support authentic, in-depth assessment
and make extended simulations particularly applicable to preprofessional programs.

Designing an Extended Simulation

As indicated earlier, any course design begins with the learning objectives or educational outcomes. The following four areas may offer goal-oriented design options for extended simulation courses:

1. Exposure to substantive issues of your discipline.
2. Application of your discipline's doctrine and theory to real-world issues.
3. Familiarity with the operation of the public and private institutions of your discipline.
4. Exercising the skills of your discipline.

Most simulations, because they require students to "do" something, combine two or more of these learning objectives. A student in a business course can simulate the role of a corporate executive developing and presenting a business plan to the board of directors. Students in an ancient history class can simulate a Greek senate debating whether to issue new taxes or to expand their nation's boundaries. Medical students can seek consensus on a difficult diagnosis during a simulated "grand rounds." In an extended simulation—again because you have the time—you can design scenarios that focus student thought and action on multiple learning objectives. Because of these various perspectives, students can not only achieve their own goals, but they can also watch classmates similarly master complex learning objectives.

Creating Scenarios

Extended simulations require you to think conceptually about dealing with several scenarios at the same time, rather than just one. This change drives many other considerations in how you design, manage, and assess an extended simulation course. First, you must assemble the group of scenarios you will use. Others may have prepared scenarios for an extended simulation course in your discipline, or you may have designed them, following the guidelines we offered in chapter 3. Whatever the source, you need to determine that (a) they will achieve the goals of your course, and (b) they will fit harmoniously together. We developed something called a scenario summary to facilitate this. The scenario summary identifies the subject matter of the scenario, its major issues, essential roles, types of activity, and learning objectives. An example appears as appendix A.

Use the scenario summary to build a platform for your simulation course that includes the right combination of substantive topics, skills, and discipline-related processes, as well as the right number and type of roles. Most scenarios can be modified to change the focus of the activities or skills with relatively little effect on the supporting documents or the environment established for the original scenario. Keeping your thumb here, turn back to chapter 2 and review where we described how a scenario involving discrimination in the workplace could be modified to focus on different substantive issues, processes, roles, and skills, depending on the course's learning objectives. And, as we describe later in this chapter, roles can be recast to accommodate any number of participants and to provide an overlap of scenarios that create a single fluid environment for an extended simulation.

After you have accumulated several scenarios covering the learning objectives of your course, you will have to choose which to use. First compare the number of students registered for your simulation course with the suggested number of roles the combined scenarios require. As we explain in the following section, each student should be assigned approximately three to five roles, with some roles having an active part in more than one scenario. You will have some flexibility to expand or narrow the activity of the roles by assigning related roles in a scenario (the board of directors, all officers, employees, and shareholders of a corporation, for example) to a single student or by assigning additional students to assist with a single role. Consider assigning several students to roles that are particularly demanding. You may assign them as a team, or, as we suggest, assign them to different but related roles, as might be typical in real life (employee, supervisor, and manager in the same business, for example).

After determining the student-role ratio, you might want to look at the reality of the scenarios. All of the simulation scenarios used in the legal capstone course were based on real events or proposed projects. Many were closely patterned on facts of appellate court cases dealing with the subject matter of the courses we were integrating. Others found their origin in current news stories or journal articles that uncovered an interesting void in existing practice or stimulated new ways to use current substantive knowledge and theories. As we have frequently emphasized, the instructor has the freedom to use the facts of an actual case or to mold new facts to suit particular instructional goals.

In selecting scenarios, you might also consider: the important issues currently being discussed by legislatures or leaders of your discipline, the accessibility of the necessary source documents, and the availability of outside experts—those persons with first-hand experience about the issues explored in your simulation who are willing to discuss them with your students.

Although well-written scenarios are usually successful if played out as intended, encourage every student to convince you of more important issues to examine or of alternative ways to achieve the identified goals. These challenges stretch students beyond the limits of existing doctrine and practice and ensure a more stimulating and rewarding experience for everyone involved. Here are some additional suggestions for designing scenarios for an extended simulation course.

Some scenarios will jump out at you, often because they are based on a case study you or the author of your course text has selected to demonstrate a substantive principle. Often, with only modest "tweaking," you can incorporate such a case into your simulated environment. By merely changing the names, the situs of the action, and the local rules relevant to the events, you can create a scenario.

In selecting and adapting a scenario, decide first whether you want students to (a) learn the application of a principle to a true-to-life situation or (b) delve deeper into the principle itself. If the former is your goal, select a scenario rich in facts and lots of characters that can play itself out in a variety of settings (negotiations, political action, business dealings, etc.). Then, design the action to move quickly through several different or sequential steps. Focus on skills such as gathering facts, identifying issues, researching, writing, giving oral presentations, and the like. Try as best you can to remove any boundaries to student actions and to encourage their experimentation. The more interstudent action that takes place, the better they will be able to hone their skills and experience the application of the discipline principles to real life. You might even consider restarting the scenario—or adding a new but similar one—during the same semester with different facts, thus allowing students a broader experience with the issue.

On the other hand, you can get your students to reach for deeper knowledge of a substantive doctrine by slowing down the pace of simulated action, while introducing more interests—and roles—to the scenario that will challenge the students to examine the issues more closely. Research, writing, and oral presentations—according to the processes of your discipline—may be more appropriate simulation activities.

Whether you are targeting application or an in-depth understanding of principles—remembering that these goals are invariably intertwined—you must help your students master essential skills, but you must also leave them free to determine—or at least influence—the ways they will achieve the essential course goals. You should rarely assign a specific path to the intended goal. Paraphrasing General George Patton, never tell people how to do something, only what to do. They will surprise you with their ingenuity.

Even though you leave students to determine pathways, you must provide scaffolding that helps them move beyond the basic skills. Basic skills, such as knowing how to gather facts, must be mastered if students did not bring them to your course. Students must know how to acquire critical information—from other students playing related roles, from talking with persons involved in the real-world process posed by the scenario, or from researching available documents and background material. They must also identify and analyze the rules and principles that affect their issue(s). After this careful review of all pertinent facts, rules, and principles, students must develop ways to further their role's interests. Extended simulations not only offer a wealth of options, but they also allow students the discretion to select the option they judge best. Often the students' personalities will affect the path they take. Students with a domineering personality may try to talk their way through the problem. A less aggressive student may attack the problem through a more formal process. Students' training and former experiences may also affect their decisions. For example, a student with work or intern experience in a related area will call on that experience or even contact past employers and supervisors. People make decisions in their lives based on similar approaches.

This necessary interaction of students gives instructors of extended simulation courses a unique ability to help students understand themselves and their peers and to develop their effective and manageable skills. You will find that you are teaching students much more than "textbook knowledge." This method of instruction continues to "bridge the gap" between academia and real-world practice. Extended simulations feature the protracted portrayal of actual practitioners in the real-world practice of the course's discipline. Simulation instructors—far from remaining aloof in the academic ivory tower—work consciously to connect their students with the professional world they will soon enter.

Whatever your discipline, identify its important processes. In our law school simulation course, we grouped our processes under the headings of: trial litigation, appellate litigation, negotiation, administrative process, legislation, and political action. If your students should be exposed to a particular process, deliberately select or slant a scenario that involves them realistically in that process. For example, one of our issues involved the cleanup of a toxic waste site. The scenario focused at various times on trial and appellate litigation, negotiations concerning the relative liabilities of parties contributing to the toxic mess, the engineering and administrative steps required to clean up the site, and the drafting of federal and state legislation to address broader substantive environmental issues. The point is that *you* control the processes your students will be exposed to.

Not every scenario will depend on a specific geographical location or legal jurisdiction for such things as local regulations, land or climate conditions, population makeup, and so on. However, for those that are, we recommend you make them the same. For some scenarios this is an easy modification—simply declare that the scenario activities take place in a specified locale. (The Pirates Landing scenario in appendix B was based on a real development in Florida. To overlap it with the scenario shown in appendix C, however, we moved it to California.) For other scenarios, you may need to get a bit more creative, for example, changing the cause of a toxic waste site from an automobile manufacturing plant in Michigan to a paint manufacturing plant in Southern California.

We recommend assigning a specific locale for several reasons. Although you can create scenario facts from your imagination, basing a scenario on an actual case and its location takes less work and adds a greater sense of reality. Also, necessary documents are easier to obtain from the site of an actual event, as are other facts that add atmosphere to the simulation environment. And finally, if your scenarios deal with laws, regulations, or public institutions, it is more realistic to use those of an actual locale.

In selecting a real situs for your simulation activities, you have two options—use the one where your school is located or use a remote one. There are pluses and minuses to each. If you place your simulation in the same geographic location as your school, your students will have ready access to many additional facts that can "flesh out" your simulation environment. As we noted in chapter 3, however, the strength of a simulation for teaching is the ability of its designer to simplify the facts to only those essential to the learning objectives. Making it too easy for students to change a scenario by adding actual facts from your location my complicate the scenario. Also, if your scenario is based on an actual case in your local area, savvy students who contact the actual participants may be tempted merely to reenact the real events rather than to reason through the process and select alternate paths. Deciding where to stage your scenarios is as complex a decision as determining the roles to build into it.

Student Roles

Four types of roles are possible in an extended simulation course, one more than in other types of educational simulations. First are the essential roles representing the central characters of the various scenarios. Students playing these roles must initiate special tasks to further the action central to your learning objectives. The students assigned these roles should be fully engaged in furthering the interests of their roles throughout the course. Next are the secondary roles in each scenario. These roles will be involved in the scenario action but are not usually responsible for initiating the action.

If a scenario were designed, for example, around an employee's claim of sexual harassment in the workplace, the most likely essential roles would be the complaining employee, the accused harasser, and a work manager. If the learning objectives of the course were the laws and legal processes involved in this situation, the essential roles would be switched to the attorneys for the two employees and a judge or mediator. In either scenario, secondary roles might be other employees (witnesses), labor union representatives, corporate officials, and government labor specialists, depending on what you want the scenario to focus. We have identified both essential roles and secondary roles in the scenarios offered in appendixes B and C. By reading these scenarios (beneath the comment balloons), you get a good idea of the differences between these role types.

Students may also assume a third type of role, the supporting bodies that will fill out your simulation environment. These could be legislators, judges, government officials, stockholders, or anyone else to whom the essential roles might go to further their interests in the scenario. These roles include the decision-making bodies you make available in your simulation. These supporting roles may be necessary because you have deliberately asked students playing essential roles to consult them. Or these roles offer reasonable optional forums available to resolve the scenario's issues. Even if you didn't originally intend or expect such a role to play a part—if you make the option available—

students in essential roles may seek on their own a decision from a classmate playing a support role.

In extended simulations a fourth type of role may emerge after the simulation begins. If the action plays out in unexpected, but rewarding ways, you can add new roles to get the most learning from this new development. Sometimes students will suggest the creation of a new role to further an interest in a way you had not anticipated. You will have to make this call at the time. You can either assign students to fill new roles, or you can simulate them yourself.

Every role requires some background information, at least enough to allow the student simulating the role to get a "feel" for it. You must then decide the amount of background needed. At one end of the spectrum, you need only to identify the role and describe its place in the scenario, allowing students to "flesh out" the background and personality based on their own past experiences and imaginations. At the other end, you can provide descriptions for each role that give a full background on the character's past involvement in the scenario situation, beliefs on issues central to the simulation subject, and motives for taking actions that you will direct. We recommend a position somewhere between these extremes. Your learning objectives will often determine the amount of information you provide. If it is important that your students experience a particular type of participant in a scenario action, be very specific. If your goal, on the other hand, is chiefly to present a "problem" and provide the typical discipline-specific mechanisms for its resolution, allow much greater latitude for your students to bring whatever character to the role they desire.

You can provide background role information for your students in several ways. One is to give them "role cards" containing whatever information you select, from general positions and interests to detailed motivation and instructions. Another is to simply turn your scenario into a story and distribute it to everyone involved, allowing students to determine on their own how they will simulate the role. (An example of this latter approach appears in appendix B.) And a third is to create a role file—hard copy or electronic—into which you place whatever background information on the role you desire, a scenario summary (in one of the forms we discuss later), and all other related documents. In this last method, students must identify on their own the relevant information and how to use it to further their roles' interests.

Advise students that they are to play all roles within the office or organization assigned to them unless other students are assigned to assist them or are assigned to simulate another role in that office. Each student should play several roles. In the management section of this chapter we discuss the number and type of roles to assign and some other pertinent factors to consider.

Instructor Role

The instructor always retains control of the operation of the simulation and the responsibility for student conduct. The instructor explains how the simulation works, when it begins, and when it ends. No two simulations are alike, and none plays out exactly as planned. It remains the instructor's task to ensure that the scenario action unfolds as well as possible and that students are achieving their learning objectives. The instructor also facilitates all of the activities and learning that occur during the debriefing sessions at the conclusion of the simulation. We have much more to say about these administrative duties of the instructor in the sections that follow on extended simulation management, debriefing, and assessment.

You must decide whether to assume a scenario role, and if so, which one(s). As mentioned earlier, many instructors who use simulations steadfastly decide not to assume a scenario role. They see students benefiting most from a simulation if they have control of it. We certainly do not disagree with this position in simple simulations with clear, straightforward instructions, roles, and activities. However, as the simulation expands, the need for guidance and control of both the scenarios and the students increases significantly. We have found that instructors can exercise this oversight if they assume the role of "supervisor" to each of the roles—or at least the essential roles—in all of the scenarios. If this oversight is unnecessary, instructors need not become directly involved. However, this decision—to participate or not to participate—is sufficiently important that you should seriously consider it in the design stage to allow for a more natural involvement later on. We say more about this later in this chapter.

Documents

Even the simplest scenarios gain verisimilitude when students receive realistic or authentic documents. These may be formal or official documents, such as employment or sales contracts, legal forms, photographs, maps, or test results, or they may be informal office memoranda, letters, phone messages, or newspaper reports. Documents serve several important functions in a simulation. They give students in their roles the necessary information to participate in the simulation. They provide background and atmosphere to the events being simulated, real or staged. They may even provide guidance to students concerning what scenario actions to take.

To save time, students can receive the appropriate documents at the outset of the simulation. You can simply place a copy of selected documents in a file maintained for each role involved in the scenario. However, as you begin to combine several scenarios in a single simulation, or if you design your scenarios as "selective and sequenced," as described later, we recommend that you keep all of your documents in a separate set of files. This approach gives you both (a) flexibility in distributing appropriate documents to the appropriate person(s) at the appropriate times and (b) control over the currency and availability of your documents as they inevitably grow in number.

This "document file" contains all of the documents available for use in all of the scenarios. The documents may be in hard copy or electronic file folders, numbered sequentially as they are filed. Students view or obtain specific documents according to the roles they are simulating. They can be directed to these documents—by you or by another simulated role—at the beginning of the simulation or at various times throughout the course. You should also encourage students to donate to the document file copies of documents they obtain or create. You should screen them carefully, however, for their accuracy and value. This source builds an ample supply of documents: After only a few semesters, you are likely to have hundreds of files. At their best, such documents may fill in information gaps or flesh out simulation scenarios; at their worst, they may be helpful to offer as "drafts" in subsequent scenarios you create.

Maintain an accurate list of all items contained in your document file. This list may or may not be shared with students. If you use computer files, consider building a keyword search capability into the system. Design a system so that multiple students will have access to the same resource documents. Whenever students remove a document from a folder, they should fill out a checkout slip that remains in the document folder. For key documents, we made multiple copies for checkout with the stipulation that students could not remove the last copy unless they were duplicating it and returning it to the folder.

By storing all role files and documents on a computer, including scenario descriptions and rules of procedures for your simulated forums, your course can be showcased over the World Wide Web and even offered for simultaneous use to classes at different schools.

Presenting the Extended Simulation

Many features make our extended simulation more than just a routine educational simulation that happens to play out over a longer period. First, and perhaps most significant, is that our extended simulation consists of several scenarios, many of which intertwine in some way. For example, a character (the leader of an activist homeowner association, for example) in a scenario that focuses on opposing increased noise from aircraft at a nearby major airport may also be a partner in a chemical company responding to allegations that it creates hazardous waste. Representatives of a national environmental group may be dealing with both of these scenarios and at the same time trying to stop construction of a housing development that is threatening both a public beach and an endangered species habitat. And the developer of that proposed housing development may also be an elected state representative who chairs the state transportation committee dealing with the need for increased aircraft flights. You can already feel the tension, can't you?

An instructor would select these scenarios because they deal with the subject matter of a single course or because they integrate several courses through their focus on relevant, substantive issues and skills. These intertwined scenarios may be modified to emphasize such things as creating regulations or legislation, filing and responding to complaints through a government agency, negotiating disputed issues, researching options for the major parties involved, or developing business plans for any commercial activities affected.

The challenge is to meld these scenarios together into the same geographic area or legislative jurisdiction, as we discussed earlier. In most cases, this merely requires some creative rewriting of the scenario facts. You must, however, pay close attention when giving parties in a single role action in more than one scenario. A goal is to assign nonconflicting interests and tasks to given roles that do not require too much activity for a single student. (Although if this does inadvertently occur you may always assign another student to act as an "associate" to share the workload.)

Regardless of how the facts, roles, and actions of your scenarios are intertwined, we now discuss two different ways of presenting integrated simulations. Which one you elect will determine to a great extent how you will manage the action in the scenarios selected. (Keep your thumb in the appendixes.)

Single-Synopsis Scenario

The single-synopsis scenario offers the simplest method of presenting, distributing, and managing a scenario during a simulation. The instructor writes a single version of the scenario—including character backgrounds, the factual setting, the problem(s) to be resolved, and the goals of each identified character. This scenario is then distributed to all students who simulate one of the characters in the scenario. An example of this scenario type appears in appendix B. This presentation method has the advantage of providing all students with all of the relevant material needed at the beginning of the simulation. Relevant files can be maintained on a computer disk, a course Web page, or in a file cabinet. Whichever distribution method you select, all documents and instructions are available to everyone at the same time.

There are some disadvantages to this method, however. Every student will know the same background and facts for all roles and will get all of the information relevant to their own role at one time. This is rarely the case in real life. Often, information is power. Learning how to acquire information is an important lesson in itself, regardless of your other learning objectives.

As our extended simulation course developed and we added new scenarios, additional documents were added to new and existing role files. This natural evolution poses another problem. If an already-used scenario is modified or, on occasion, eliminated from a subsequent course, the accumulated documents and work products of earlier role players can burden new students with irrelevant and possibly misleading information. Make a sincere effort to avoid unproductive student work in this fast-paced instructional method. Accordingly, you must examine each role file to ensure that it contains all of the relevant documents but not unnecessary ones.

Mindful of these problems, we recommend this type of simulation scenario for instructors who are creating their first extended simulation course, or if the course contains only a few scenarios. Its primary advantages are ease of administration and continuing instructor control.

Selective and Sequenced Scenario

The selective and sequenced scenario approach is characterized by four ways to present information to students. First, not all students receive the same information. Each student receives only that information the instructor determines the character would actually know. In some scenarios, the characters are intentionally given different and even conflicting information if the instructor feels this would better resemble real life. Students playing various roles, for example, might "hear" a conversation differently or rely on different measurements or figures. To find missing information, the characters must discover it from each other. And determining what information is correct is often an object of the scenario.

Second, information sequencing differs in a selective and sequenced scenario. Students in various roles receive general background information first with more detailed facts offered later. This approach resembles real life more closely by building the amount of information, training, and experience a character would receive over a simulated time of weeks, months, or years. This approach also emphasizes the compressed simulation time the students must work within. Selective sequencing of information increases the complexity of the simulation considerably. To minimize problems, the scenario designer and instructor (if they are different individuals) must be able to anticipate with reasonable accuracy the sequence and speed of the normal development of the scenario activities, both in real life and as a simulation.

Third, through a numbered document file, the instructor distributes to students—at various times throughout the simulation—specific documents and directions. The instructor then specifies—if desired—the appropriate time to review specific documents. For example, if students playing certain roles need to learn how to prepare a contract, an important learning objective, you might first show them a similar contract, ask then to identify the specific contract terms to include, and require a "draft" of the document as a graded event. After the students submit the proposed contract(s), you can review and correct it before all interested parties use it during the rest of the scenario. Students thus receive documents you have prepared in advance, but only as the scenario unfolds. Thus, their learning is based on a scaffold approach.

By controlling the amount and the timing of information available to participants, you eliminate the "knowledge gap" we discussed in chapter 3. Too much information at one time manipulates students and limits their learning on their own. Too little information may leave them floundering needlessly, missing the learning objectives completely and becoming frustrated.

Last, in both types of simulations, either the single-synopsis or selected and sequenced, each student is given specific tasks to accomplish for each of the roles assigned. These may be either general tasks (discuss possible remedies to airport noise problems) or specific tasks (file a lawsuit seeking damages for nuisance by Simulation Day 7). In a sequenced scenario presentation, these tasks are given in a realistic—and sequenced—manner. To avoid (unintended) conflicts, care must be taken to cross-check the tasks against different characters in the same scenario and for the same character in different scenarios. This method of assigning tasks allows the instructor greater control over the pace of the simulation and a greater ability to track the progress of each student. Selecting the tasks you will assign to students in their various roles drives the flow of the scenarios.

The vehicle we recommend to accomplish this sequenced distribution of information and tasks is the "office memorandum," distributed to the students, by role, on preselected "simulation days." Once again, the instructor must have some familiarity with how the scenario would most likely play out in real life to rationally sequence the action for students. All of the memoranda for the roles and scenarios selected for the course may then be assembled and sorted ahead of time for distribution on the appropriate simulation day. An example of this method of scenario presentation appears in appendix C. Let us take a moment now to explain the separate elements of this scenario design. The first element is the scenario plan. This is similar to the scenario summary in appendix A, but is adapted to each execution of the scenario— who is to play which roles, what documents will be required, what processes will be highlighted, and so on. The second element—the guide—is the scenario story, broken down by essential role and sequenced by simulation day. The guide also contains directions to the students playing various roles. It tells them to obtain certain documents and to perform specific tasks to further the interests of each essential role. Next is a list of the tasks assigned to each of the essential roles—with space to note the time each task was performed and the performance level of the student in accomplishing the task. This feature is invaluable both for tracking the progress of the scenario action and for assigning grades. The list of tasks is simply "cut and pasted" from the guide section of the scenario. The last element consists of the instructional memoranda for students in each role, prepared in advance but not distributed until a preselected simulation day. Again, these memoranda are simply cut and pasted from the guide onto a formatted memorandum document. The actual distribution can be accomplished by handing out hard copy memoranda, e-mailing them to students, or making them available to selected students at specific times on a course Web page.

Creating the Extended Simulation Environment

How you set up your simulation environment—those features that add to the reality you want your students to feel during the simulation—will dictate to a great extent how you will be able to manage the actual simulation activity once it gets going. At the same time, decisions you make on how involved you want to become in managing the action of this simulation—closely or loosely or not at all—will influence how you should design your simulation environment. Designing an extended simulation environment and managing the simulation are completely interrelated. As always, your learning objectives will shape the simulation action, which is regulated by both the environment you create and how you manage the action. Just as we suggested you read chapters 3 and 4 "back and forth" to understand this interrelationship, we recommend that you consider together this next section on creating an extended simulation environment and the following section on managing extended simulations.

An extended education simulation is designed to replicate selected aspects of the real world. Two widely used methods of teaching students in an actual real-world environment are internships and clinics under the supervision of university faculty. Although we enthusiastically support these teaching methods, we note two significant drawbacks in their use. The first is timing. Rarely can an actual case present itself and play out to a conclusion in the course of a semester. In our extended simulation, however, compression of time not only allows you to explore the full range of issues and activities involved, but you can also have students deal with these issues at any stage of the actual process. Furthermore, you can—as we have done—reinforce or augment learning by having students replay the same scenario with altered facts or through different processes.

The second reason dealing with actual cases can be limiting is because real people are involved. You cannot take risks with someone's life, even to underscore an important teaching point! On the other hand, a simulation course allows students to choose ways to resolve conflicts and achieve goals without the associated risks. To achieve this realism, however, you must create a full environment with all the necessary props and machinery. Abstract knowledge alone is not enough. Your graduates must go beyond the latest trends in your substantive field or the latest decisions, legislation, inventions, or scientific breakthroughs. They must also know the environment within which to achieve the results they want, or at least the results their clients, patients, or employers will accept. This means knowing something about the institutions and people responsible for dealing with their issues.

If, for example, your students, upon graduation, will have to deal with the problem of toxic wastes, shipping of hazardous materials, or commercial development in a coastal zone, in addition to knowing federal and state laws, they must know how the Environmental Protection Agency (EPA) is organized, who the decision makers are in their region, what role the National Oceanic and Atmospheric Administration (NOAA) plays, how rule makers make and apply regulations, and how to work with the local environmental agents who are most likely to influence their interests. In the field of business, your graduates will be successful only if they know who the business players are—public and private—and how to guide their business proposal through the wickets to final approval. This involves getting public and staff support for a proposal, negotiating trade-offs, planning and conducting meetings, and dealing with the media.

To prepare your students to do this later in real practice, populate your simulated community with the same diverse collection of public and private organizations and people they will meet upon graduation. A simulation course allows students to learn about and experience the makeup, procedures, and interests of these organizations while they seek to achieve the goals you have set for them. Physical space, time, decision-making bodies, and a community news outlet shape the environment within which the simulated community is built.

The Classroom

You can run an extended simulation from a single classroom, but you should arrange for it to be dedicated exclusively to your course during the semester. Students will need to have as much access to it as possible, which is another argument for setting up as much of your simulation as you can on a course Web page. For now, we offer some ideas on how you can transform your classroom—and other spaces—into the physical space your simulation environment needs to get students engaged.

Consider the activities you expect to occur and how your classroom can accommodate them. Do what you can to your classroom(s) to give your simulation the proper feel and atmosphere. If you have designed scenario activities that will take place in a boardroom or conference room, encourage students to move tables and chairs together to appear like a board room. Even better would be to arrange access to an actual conference room in your department. If you have built in courtroom activities, give some thought to transforming your classroom, or another room in the school, into a courtroom setting. The same holds true for office discussions (allow students to use your office, perhaps), public meetings (a student lounge), or demonstrations (an area outside your class building). Often it does not take much physical rearrangement to achieve the desired environment—just a good imagination. And, given permission, you will be delighted to see your students wholeheartedly jump into this activity.

Like the starkly designed theater production we mentioned earlier, the attitude with which your students play their roles will do more to set the environment for your simulation than scenery. However, every effort to create a realistic environment is worthwhile. In addition to rearranging tables and chairs, consider adding some props to the activity to help set the scene. For instance, you can give judicial robes to judges and have students wear appropriate business clothes to meetings or legislative sessions.

In the section on managing an extended simulation, we suggest that you construct a "simulation center," either a physical room or a separate space on a course Web page. We also explain what should go into this simulation center

Simulation Time

As we have emphasized several times, by accelerating the flow of events in your simulation to occur at a faster-than-normal pace, you eliminate most of the "dead time" lost in actual cases and force students to initiate and respond to actions very quickly. In addition, this acceleration has the collateral learning objective of assuring that students will experience the time pressures of real-life practice. You can get a sense of this accelerated pace of activities by scanning the information given and the tasks required in the sample selective and sequenced scenario in appendix C.

Besides adding to the sense of reality, compression of time allows students to develop a plan of action, implement it, and see the results of their choices during a one-semester course. If the action of a scenario is initiated quickly enough, a compressed-time simulation will allow for appeals of lost trials, the reorganization of a bankrupt business, the miraculous cure of a potentially lethal disease, and even the passage of legislation to solve problems after other means have failed.

The ratio of simulation time to real time can be fixed at any value you desire. We found that *3 to 4 years* is long enough to encompass most of the events leading to a solution of our problems and is short enough to seem realistic. We also found it best to start the simulation time approximately 2 years earlier than the actual time. During a one-semester course, this will take the simulation through the present time and slightly into the future. While most of the background time is passing, students are learning their roles, gathering facts, and planning their strategies. A sample comparison chart of real time to simulation time for a one-semester course that meets twice a week is presented in table 7.1.

To force students to focus on this passage of time, we do not allow the use of actual court or administrative decisions, inventions, or legislation before the corresponding simulation time. Students may "look into the future" and use the arguments of "future" cases and laws, but the holdings are not binding. This manipulation of time also gives both instructors and students the opportunity to "rewrite" actual events and go beyond them with new decisions, inventions, legislation, and so forth.

Decision-Making Bodies

Using an extended simulation allows students the time to decide for themselves how to further the interests of the roles they are simulating. The extra time allows them to make choices and to observe and deal with the consequences of their choices. But these consequences may mean that students playing other roles oppose the actions they select. In such cases, they need to have available the mechanisms to resolve the inevitable conflicts created by the options they decide on. Thus, they need decision-making bodies.

Create or simulate your discipline's decision-making bodies—such as a court, board of directors, review board, administrative agency, and the like—and assign students to fill these support roles as part of your simulated environment. Even if such bodies and their procedures are not a part of your syllabus, consider adding some to your extended simulation. Many of your simulations will have built-in conflicts among parties, but even if not initially present, competing interests may escalate into conflict.

Table 7.1		
Real Time—Simulation Time Conversion		
Real Date	**Simulation Day**	**Simulation Date**
Mon. Aug. 21		Orientation; distribute instructions
Thur. Aug. 24		Comments by "alumni," tour simulation center
Mon. Aug. 28	Day 1	Assign roles; distribute scenarios; START simulation
Thur. Aug. 31	Day 2	Mar. 1, (current year −2)
Mon. Sept. 4	No Class—Labor Day: May 1, (current year −2)	
Thur. Sept. 7	Day 3	July 1, (current year −2) Log #1 due
Mon. Sept. 11	Day 4	Sept. 1, (current year −2)
Thur. Sept. 14	Day 5	Nov. 1, (current year −2) Log #2 due
Mon. Sept. 18	Day 6	Jan. 1, (current year −1)
Thur. Sept. 21	Day 7	Mar. 1, (current year −1) Log #3 due
Mon. Sept. 25	Day 8	May 1, (current year −1)
Thur. Sept. 28	Day 9	July 1, (current year −1) Log #4 due
Mon. Oct. 2	Admin. Day	Debriefing
Thur. Oct. 5	Day 10	Sept. 1, (current year −1) Log #5 due
Mon. Oct. 9	Day 11	Nov. 1, (current year −1)
Thur. Oct. 12	Day 12	Jan. 1, (current year) Log #6 due
Mon. Oct. 16	Day 13	Mar. 1, (current year)
Thur. Oct. 19	Day 14	May 1, (current year) Log #7 due
Mon. Oct. 23	Day 15	July 1, (current year)
Thur. Oct. 26	Day 16	Sept. 1, (current year) Log #8 due
Mon. Oct. 30	Day 17	Nov. 1, (current year)
Thur. Nov. 2	Admin. Day	Debriefing
Mon. Nov. 6	Day 18	Jan. 1, (current year +1) Log #9 due
Thur. Nov. 9	Day 19	Mar. 1, (current year +1)
Mon. Nov. 13	Day 20	May 1, (current year +1) Log #10 due
Thur. Nov. 16	Day 21	July 1, (current year + 1) End of Simulation
Mon. Nov. 20	Final Log #11 due: Simulation Debriefing	
Thur. Nov. 23	No Class—Thanksgiving	
Mon. Nov. 27	Simulation Debriefing	
Thur. Nov. 30	Final Debriefing	

These conflicts need to be resolved—in a manner best resembling reality—without your serving as the decision maker and without putting it to chance (the role of a die, for example). If your course involves such a decision-making body, consider requiring the students using it to closely follow its actual procedural rules. If not, develop some simple procedural rules to allow the characters in your simulation to reach a realistic decision. The availability of these decision-making bodies is often more important than the actual processes: You make that judgment call. We offer three common examples of such decision-making bodies.

Simulation Courts   A legal forum gives students an effective means through which they can propose and challenge new ideas, whether legal, medical, social, or business related. To accomplish this, create your own court system, using students as judges and counsel. With the help of our law students, we drafted rules of trial and appellate court procedure for civil and criminal courts, as well as a small claims court. You can pattern rules after those of your state court or, as we did, after the federal court.

We recommend that you construe procedural matters liberally, with a view to protecting the rights of the parties against mistake, inadvertence, surprise, or neglect. The intent should be to afford students a decision-making forum, not to get them bogged down in procedural hairsplitting. Nevertheless, all time-driven filing requirements must be strictly enforced—the semester simply goes by too quickly. Once students learn these requirements will be enforced, they will quickly abide by them. You cannot, however, anticipate all situations that will arise. Our advice is to let your student-judges resolve them to the best of their ability. The learning point will sink in, regardless of the outcome. Likewise, if a student is able to explain how an actual court rule would allow relief where one of your simulated rules would not, you might have your judges grant the relief. We found that this encourages students to learn the actual rules of the tribunal before which they will practice.

Simulation court rules must take into account the compressed time of your simulation and the need to quickly and easily move through the court processes. We suggest that you allow a party 48 hours (real time) to answer complaints and 24 hours (real time) to reply to motions. Parties should state all claims in their complaint and all defenses and counterclaims in their answer. In our course, Saturdays and Sundays were not included in the calculation of any time period for court rules.

All parties should be required to stipulate (agree to facts not in dispute) to the fullest extent possible. And simulation judges should schedule pretrial conferences within 10 real days from the filing of a complaint. At these conferences, the parties should submit a joint pretrial statement that includes: a list of all witnesses and evidence each expects to present, stipulated facts and those in dispute, a statement of legal issues, each party's theory of the case, and all authorities relied on. Judges should have weekly calendar calls to review the status of their assigned cases, press for settlement, and keep the parties to strict timelines.

We encourage you to use trials before only a judge, but if you allow juries, we recommend that they consist of three persons, with a finding of a majority of two taken as a finding by the jury. Jurors are also examples of support roles we mentioned earlier. If you assign several students as judges, those not assigned as a judge in a particular case can act as jurors.

If you decide to use a court as part of your simulation course for any of the reasons we outlined in chapter 4, you will need a simple and efficient method to file documents and make court records available to the parties of the suit, your judges, and the public. We recommend simply having two files for each case in your simulation center. One will be a public file open to the parties and to the public. Parties file their own documents in the public file. A second, or court file, is open only to your simulation judges. A copy of all papers filed is placed in a separate judges' box, and the student assigned as chief judge or court clerk files the papers in the appropriate case folder in the court file. The court file may also contain copies of relevant cases and statutes relied on, previous court rulings and analyses, judges' notes, and helpful hints from the instructor.

To file a complaint or appeal, the plaintiff/appellant assigns the next available case number to his or her action—determined from a list (court docket) of all cases displayed in the simulation center—and places copies of the complaint/appeal in both the judges' box and the public file. The plaintiff must also serve a copy of the complaint/appeal on the defendant/appellee, either by personally giving him or her a copy or by putting it into that person's mailbox. All other court documents are filed and served in the same manner.

In one of our law school simulations, students filed 70 cases. Of these, 28 were settled, 9 went to trial, 3 were appealed, 13 resulted in dismissals, and 17 were not heard within the term (semester) of the court. Among the issues dealt with by our simulation court system were: breach of contract, home foreclosure, bankruptcy, assault, EPA toxic waste cleanup, labor suit against an employer, damages from airplane noise, First Amendment claim to allow a religious group to hand out literature at an airport, breach of manufacturer warranty, and tortious negligence in handling hazardous wastes. There is no way this scope of substantive or litigation issues could have been addressed in a lecture course or a legal practice clinic. Those directly involved in these simulated trials claimed to have learned a great deal, and during the debriefing, we concluded the same.

Your simulation court and its associated rules of procedure may be more or less complex than ours, depending on the legal education and experience of your students. However, even those with no legal education or experience can gain substantially by participating in a simple simulation court.

Simulation Legislature Another effective and realistic forum within which your students may play out their scenarios is a legislature. Legislative bodies may be adapted to your teaching objectives, and the legislative processes—from public hearings to committee meetings to voting on a bill—are familiar enough to most students to allow them to promote their interests and to seek solutions to their problems in a realistic fashion.

In simulation classes of less than 20 students or for simulations that cover only a few class sessions, we recommend using a single unicameral legislative body. All students should be assigned as a representative of an area or state and should be instructed either to determine the position of the actual sitting legislator for issues that come before the simulated legislature or to represent the interests assigned to them in their roles. Appoint a president pro tempore and majority and minority leaders and task them with forming committees and assigning proposed legislation dealing with the scenario issues.

Each class day should begin with a legislative day. After ascertaining if a quorum is present, your legislature should follow a prescribed order of business. Ours was: messages from the president/governor, reports from department heads, reports from committees, unfinished business, and the introduction of new bills and resolutions. New bills had two readings, one on the day the bill was introduced. They were then referred to a committee and generally followed a standard legislative process. Limited time was allowed for debate, and voting followed standard procedures.

The idea and incentive to propose most legislation comes from the tasks you assign students playing selected roles in your scenarios. However, the legislature is available to any participant of the simulation to lobby and seek passage of helpful legislation. You will have to develop abbreviated rules for proposing and adopting legislation, similar to the court rules mentioned earlier.

In simulation courses with more than 20 students and that run the entire semester, you should consider having both a state and national legislative body. Again, unicameral bodies for both work best in this short time frame. We recommend making the rules of procedure the same or similar, unless your teaching objectives call for more distinctive or realistic differences.

Administrative Agency   No matter what your discipline, a governmental or quasi-governmental agency will likely at some level deal with your issues. Such an agency can be used as a decision-making body to hold hearings and make rulings on disputes arising from your scenario actions. As with courts and legislative bodies, you can craft practice procedures for these agencies as simple or complex (real) as your learning objectives call for. Assign students to simulate the roles of the decision makers of these agencies, give them their operating rules, and allow them to act as they judge best. An alternative is to ask sitting or retired officials from such agencies to fill these roles. We discuss this option more fully later in this chapter.

The Simulation News

We found it extremely helpful to publish a course newspaper. It allows the instructor to add background flavor to individuals, organizations, and events in the scenarios. You may use real articles from the stories your scenarios are based on as well as relevant, fictitious articles. The paper can also be used for publication of legal notices for all manner of things. And it is useful for dissemination of information to students, whether the information relates to a scenario or to class administration. A simulation course newspaper also serves as a vehicle for expressing public interest in or opposition to political candidates, proposed legislation, business plans, scientific discoveries, or anything else the "characters" of the simulation consider relevant.

Your newspaper can be distributed as a hard copy edition, sent through e-mail, or posted on a course Web page. Each student acts as reporter and editor, preparing articles, photos, and cartoons "camera ready" for copying. Only the instructor can censor articles, but even here you should consider exercising restraint. In one extended simulation course, a student "published" an article attacking another student (obviously, in the role portraying a conflicting interest), and the "newspaper" was sued for libel. This was entirely unplanned but became one of the more instructive features of that course.

We recommend that you have on hand a supply of general-interest articles, cartoons, and letters to the editor to "prime the pump" until students get into the feel of their characters. Be mindful, of course, of copyright laws for "fair use." Many of these articles can be prepared in advance and others may be prompted by the actions (or inaction) of your students. We published our newspaper once a week during a regular semester course. A sample of *The Simulation News* we "published" is in appendix D.

Students from Other Programs

The number of students you admit to the course from other disciplines will proportionately improve your simulation course and give its environment a completely different feel—ideally one more approximating the actual environments you are simulating in your scenarios. In our land use course, students from the planning school worked excellently as local government officials. They got valuable experience working with our student "attorneys" and managing the sort of work they would be handling after graduation. Business students added realism to many of the commercial activities of our course. And a journalism student will learn a lot if allowed to investigate for and publish *The Simulation News*.

Managing Extended Simulations

In this section, we offer suggestions to manage your extended simulation course. These suggestions begin with gathering information about your students and selecting scenarios before the first class and continue through the simulation activity itself. They conclude with post simulation modifications. Planning is essential for a smooth-running course, but overplanning or overcontrol can be detrimental to your students' learning. The excitement of this type of course is created by its unpredictability. Allow your students to select and open doors on their own. Their creativity and enthusiasm will astound you and will provide them with the learning experiences you seek.

After you decide you will try an extended simulation for your course, schedule a meeting with your dean or department head. After you have won your case for such a course, try to obtain as many of the following concessions as possible. Request a separate room for the exclusive use of your simulation students as a simulation center and request the use of a conference room or additional classroom for periodic simulation activities. Request a teaching or research assistant to help you manage, observe, and evaluate the many simulation activities that will take place at the same time. This assistant can also help prepare and distribute documents, file papers, publish the simulation newspaper, check student logs, and assist students in finding and copying necessary scenario documents. A second choice is giving academic credit to a student who has taken the extended simulation course before and can serve as an assistant. As a third option, try to get a volunteer to help.

Request permission from your dean or registrar to require students to read a description of your extended simulation course before registering and to complete a data card upon registration. Student participation is critical to this course, and you must do all you can to explain what the course involves and what is expected of students who register for it. A typical one-paragraph explanation in a curriculum handbook is not adequate. The data card should list students' past education, employment, and experience. Do not limit this to areas related to the subject matter of your course. Also solicit prospective students' interests in the types of work they hope to pursue upon graduation. Collect these data cards before your first class and use the information in assigning roles.

We offer some suggestions later concerning whom to assign to the essential roles in your scenarios. However, we suggest that for all role assignments you also consider assigning students to roles opposite the interests they express. Their experience or interest in the topic of the scenario will get them quickly engaged in the action, and requiring them to represent the other side very often brings out their most imaginative and productive efforts.

Let potential students know that this course will require them to attend every class and will require a great amount of time outside of class to work with other students. Also solicit in advance the degree of certainty each student has for completing your simulation course. Once the simulation has begun, any drops from the course create a disruptive ripple effect on other students. This information will help you avoid assigning key roles to students likely to drop.

Assigning Essential Roles

Pay particular attention to assigning students to the essential roles. Review the student data cards and select the best candidates on the basis of education and experience. If possible, interview students before the first day of class to select the obvious leaders and avoid placing students with weak personalities into leadership roles. The essential roles in our legal simulation and the factors we considered in filling them were:

1. *Legislative leaders:* Work experience counts more than grades. If you don't have a student with legislative experience, student government experience will help. A strong personality is required to persuade others to become involved in the legislative process of the simulation course and to keep order during legislative sessions.

2. *Chief judge:* Select someone with mock trial courtroom experience or at least with experience in debating. This person must be able to take charge of other students, make on-the-spot decisions, and have a strong personality to demand adherence to strict time limitations by parties to a suit. Other judges should also possess these qualities. A rule of thumb is one judge for every 10 students to spread the workload. These students serve as all types of judges (civil, criminal, family court, and administrative) and at all levels (trial and appellate).

3. *Political leaders:* These are roles for people who must assess the interests of their constituencies and make decisions on policies and plans for the future. They must also be capable of marshalling proposed legislation through whatever process wickets you set up. As with real

politicians, an outgoing personality rises to the top of the qualifications. However, it is just as important to select students with differing personal views or the ability to convincingly advocate a variety of views.

4. *Business leaders:* Whether your roles are public or private sector, some business experience and education is important to accurately portray these roles and run their activities realistically.

5. *Heads of citizen groups:* Student leaders, organizers, and activists of all types are great for these roles. To bring life to the simulation, these students must play their characters with passion.

We found it best to assign several roles to each student, involving them in different scenarios. Not only will this multiple assignment expose each student to more substantive issues and processes, but it will also expose students to the ideas and actions of many more students. As in real life, students will be able to pick up on positive experiences in one scenario and transfer them to another. Exposure to various scenarios also gives each student a view of the larger simulation environment you have created and typically gets them thinking "outside the box." In addition to any that you have planned, alliances will form among students according to their roles and the interests they are championing in various scenarios. It is often from these alliances that unplanned, but extremely valuable, teaching moments arise.

As a rule of thumb, assign each student three to five roles. One or two of the roles should be major characters who will initiate considerable activity during the course or be on the receiving end of such activity from several fronts. The remaining secondary roles should be peripheral roles in other scenarios. Be advised that actual role activity levels do not always develop at the pace or to the extent anticipated. Experience with simulations counts here. Keep in mind that you can always add an underworked student to the "staff" of an overworked student or even reassign a role to a different student.

Unless you have a specific reason to give students limited or focused experiences during the simulation course, we suggest mixing role types for most students to afford some exposure to each of the following:

essential and supporting roles,

public and private interests,

initiator of and responder to scenario action, and

varied process types (research, writing, negotiation, administrative, etc.).

Be careful, however, not to assign roles to students that will conflict with other interests they have in other roles or scenarios. Additionally, try to anticipate the periods demanding the greatest activities for each role and avoid overloading students with competing responsibilities.

Do your best, but do not worry too much about role assignments the first time you use the extended simulation method. You can easily recast students as the semester progresses to avoid role conflicts and to balance workloads. To quote an old cliché: "Experience is the best teacher."

Instructor Roles

Earlier, we commented on the issues you should consider in deciding whether you will take any direct involvement in the simulation and, if so, what roles you might assume. At the very least, you will have to continue the role of instructor, telling students when the simulation begins, getting class started each day, and dealing with student issues (missing class, allegations of cheating, and so forth.) Although it will help if you continue to exercise, as needed, your authority as instructor, for the sake of changing the environment and atmosphere from a regular classroom to an extended education simulation, we suggest that you define a new instructor role for yourself.

You do not need to assume any simulation role. If a scenario issue arises, you may simply tell the students to take care of it themselves. Although this will clearly present a learning opportunity, we suggest against it. The events in the simulation move quickly. To get the most learning out of your simulation, try to maintain whatever momentum your students generate. For this reason, we suggest that although you should avoid writing yourself into any essential role, you should be prepared to assume a scenario role whenever needed.

We further suggest that—only when needed—you take the role of a senior partner or a supervisor of any role where a student legitimately seeks assistance. Your job would then be to advise the junior associates (students) in your office and ensure they are doing their jobs. You do not need to know more about the technical details of a scenario than a senior executive might. Your value is to assess the soundness of the student's plan, challenge it with other ideas, and help students explore alternatives. If you are not an expert in the subject matter of the scenario, the scenario summaries will provide a reliable framework. On the other hand, if you do have experience with the substantive or procedural issues, you will bring that insight to the simulation.

Alternatively, you should consider asking other professors, practitioners, or public officials to assist by participating in the course or by being "on call" to students. Our experience has shown that practitioners are uncommonly willing to give freely of their time and experience and are a constant source of support for our students. Consider asking practitioners in the areas represented by your scenario roles to participate in the simulation by playing their real-life roles, such as business executives, hearing examiners, local officials, and so forth. If they do not have the time to prepare for such involvement, ask if they would be willing to observe a simulated proceeding before students playing their role and offer comments at its conclusion. They will enjoy this contact with students and will become a source of information and up-to-date documents for future scenarios. They may also be potential employers of some of your students.

Faculty members, too, can be good resources. Many faculty members are unfamiliar with simulation teaching, so you will need to orient them. Some may also have limited practical experience with the discipline you are teaching. Nevertheless, you should solicit their assistance; their cooperation can be invaluable. First, offer your scenarios for their review and ask them to comment on issues of substantive doctrine, factual development, and practice techniques within their areas of interest. Then, see if they will allow your students to ask them questions within their areas of expertise. You might even work toward a joint course with them. If they are receptive at all, ask them if they would be willing to play a role, one that offers advice or guidance to students, in one or more of your scenarios.

Capitalizing—sometimes unexpectedly—on the talent of local practitioners and faculty members underscores the need for flexibility and fluidity. As we have noted, the instructor must maintain the power to change facts, roles, rules, and tasks to benefit the learning process of the simulation. Students may drop the course, become overloaded, or have their characters in the scenario effectively preempted by the way the action develops. The instructor can change the flow of the simulation as necessary to change student involvement or for pedagogic reasons.

If the flow of the simulation suggests that you should assume a role, try your best to portray that role as accurately as possible. Many former students have stated that they often relied on their experiences in our simulation course to get them started professionally or to help them perform effectively in the position they acquired upon graduation. Their model for their own behavior was often a role that the instructor filled in our extended simulation course.

One final thought on the instructor's role. We strongly suggest that, when assuming a role in a scenario, your students address you as they would in the context of that scenario. This might involve calling you by your first name or by "sir or ma'am." This nomenclature adds to the professional atmosphere you are trying to achieve.

Classroom Activities

The classroom becomes a stage in an extended simulation course. Like a stage, its setting changes from scene to scene and may even have multiple acts going on at once. Each class day the simulation begins as though you are in the conference room of your various simulated offices. You, as the "senior partner," make necessary administrative announcements and open the floor for late-breaking news flashes that were unable to be printed in *The Simulation News.*

Immediately thereafter, the scene changes and the classroom becomes whichever legislative body is scheduled to sit in assembly that day. Next, the scene shifts to those hearings that you determine all students should observe. Then students are released to conduct whatever activities they feel necessary. During this time, the room may be a boardroom, a courtroom, or a local agency's staff offices—usually at the same time in different corners of the classroom. Students quickly learn that they often have to be in two places at once. How to prioritize and handle these situations is another great life lesson. To instill some order into this academic theater, we recommend that you assign regular seating for your students, grouping them by related major roles. We also recommend scheduling at least one additional classroom for these activities, but if you can't, students will find a place on their own. In one class, a legislative committee held a public hearing at 7:00 a.m. in a corner of the university coffee shop.

As both instructor and "senior partner," you will be besieged by your junior associates for a more detailed explanation of events and for guidance on where to begin. Treat these students as you would junior associates—professionally, quickly, and outside the hearing of others. This is best accomplished by setting up an "office" in a corner of the classroom and requiring brief "appointments" to see you. You will also need time to observe as many of the activities as you can. Expect to be very busy during scheduled class periods. In fact, expect to be very busy at other times as well, including at home—to the extent you allow your students to contact you at home. Because of its ready availability, e-mail has become both a blessing and a curse. Handling the increased communication flow becomes another justification for a research or teaching assistant.

At the outset, most students will be uncomfortable with the lack of direction they receive from you. Continually reinforce the point that they *should* feel this way. But you can also assure them that their uneasiness will evaporate in direct proportion to the amount of effort they expend playing their roles and attempting to find solutions to their assigned tasks.

To briefly remind you of a point we made in chapter 4, during the conduct of the simulation you have to deal with participants in three ways. Treat them as a person with individual issues such as a conflicting work schedule. Treat them as a student seeking to learn and to earn a good grade. And treat them as the professional character in their simulated role, looking for ways to advance the role interests. Each requires a different approach.

The Simulation Center

A simulation center is whatever and wherever you make it. In addition to your classroom, it will become a focal point of your course. The center is where students get information, file papers, exchange notes with other students, and play out much of the course's activities. The early versions of the simulation course on which we are basing this book occurred long before students began to use computers, the Internet, and e-mail. These technological innovations, plus the rapidly improving software products for Web page development, have exponentially enhanced your ability to set up a simulation center. You can manage your course with a little or a great deal of computer support, but we encourage you to continue to require significant student-to-student contact—the most beneficial aspect of the entire course.

We will attempt to "blend" into our description of a simulation center a physical room and its hard copy files with a Web or computer-based "room" and its electronic files. Read into the following descriptions whichever appeals to you or whichever you are able to support. Regardless, it is essential that a separate "room" be assigned to your simulation course. This room will contain the files, "public offices," and student mailboxes necessary to run an extended simulation. Students should have access to this room at all times (or at least the times your school is open). Once you have constructed this simulation center, consider giving a memorandum to each student explaining its features and establishing your rules for its use. (Ours is in appendix G.) We additionally asked a few students who had received special training to conduct "tours" of the simulation center during the first 2 days of the course.

Each student should be assigned a mail slot or folder in the simulation center. The instructor uses these "mailboxes" to distribute scenarios, documents, newspapers articles, and memoranda. They are also used by other students for delivery of documents and announcements of meetings and to pass on class-related messages. Students must check their mailboxes each class day, and no one may look at or remove anything from another student's mailbox without permission.

If you use decision-making bodies in your simulation, try to establish a separate "office" for participants to file papers and to obtain forms, documents, and rules of procedure for each forum you set up. A good place for this is in the simulation center, accessible to everyone.

The Simulation News

We previously discussed how "publishing" a simulation newspaper promotes the feeling that your simulation course is a community all its own. Such a "newspaper" also provides you a wonderful management tool. If a student in one of the roles did not pick up on an important piece of information, you can provide a gentle "reminder" in your newspaper. You and any simulation characters may use the paper to announce meetings or to report the results of meetings or legislative action, and so forth. These publications not only give recognition to those who worked on the event(s), but they also advise everyone of what is going on in the simulated community.

You may also use this means of communication for all manner of administrative issues. Some of these may be associated directly with the simulation (reminders of due dates or formats for student logs), or they may focus on school events and requirements (reminding everyone to clean up their pizza boxes from the student lounge after a simulation meeting).

Student Logs

As recommended in chapter 6 for assessment purposes, students should be required to submit an account of their activities at least once a week. This requirement will be a constant reminder to them to stay on top of their tasks and their roles' interests. It will also give you another essential means to monitor the progress of all of the scenarios.

All students should be required to follow a very specific format for the student log. This consistency allows you to quickly assess each student's activities. By comparing the student logs against role taskings and scenario summaries, you will be able to stimulate action or make midcourse changes if the action goes awry. They also provide a quick and effective means for periodic feedback (debriefing) to each student. An example of our format is in appendix E.

These student logs are helpful in grading student performance in the course. However, stress to the students that good grades are earned by the quality of their submissions, not the quantity of paper alone. Students should include with their logs a narrative of their efforts, copies of work products, notes of meetings, and responses to specific tasks. They should also share their thoughts about how they see the scenario developing, their plans for future action, and any problems they have encountered. Just as you might in a real office, you can guide your "associates'" work with a short memorandum or e-mail.

Tasks

If you follow our selected and sequenced method of designing and presenting scenarios, we hope you also build into the scenarios the specific tasks to be accomplished, at least by those in essential roles. These tasks direct students to the learning objectives you have built into the scenarios. Based on your own experience, both in real life and in these educational simulations, you should be able to predict not only what actions certain roles should take (or at least the most likely options) but also when that action should be taken and completed.

We suggest that you keep a list—by scenario—of each of the tasks required of each role in that scenario. You can build this list by simply "cutting and pasting" the tasks from your scenario plan. (See ours in appendix C.) Then as students report their weekly activity, by role, in their student logs, you can compare it with the task list to see if all is going well. If not, simply give another memorandum to tardy students to urge them into action. We recommend that you use "simulation day," as shown in table 7.1, as your time line for assigning due dates for tasks. This task list will again prove helpful when it comes time to assess student performance in your simulation course.

To disseminate relevant information about what is happening in each of the scenarios, we suggest that each head of a decision-making body (legislature, board, court, union, etc.) be required to publish a record of official actions taken. This can be published in *The Simulation News,* thumbtacked to a bulletin board, posted on a Web page, or announced in open class. Here again, balance simplicity with actual publication requirements; your goal is to "get the word out." An example of one we used quite a bit is our report from the chief judge of our simulation courts. Practitioners in real life must keep abreast of litigation in which they or their clients have an interest. The same is true in your simulation course. To assist all parties, our chief judge published an updated court report at least weekly. This report contained a list of all complaints filed, the general nature of the case, orders issued, and the final resolution. The point was to help students stay aware of anything going on that might affect one of their roles in a scenario. Such a list will also help you monitor the development of the scenarios.

Starting the Simulation

On the first day of class introduce the simulation process and explain the policies of your "office," the physical environment, and the requirement for student logs. To set the correct mood at the outset, we recommend that much of this information be given to your students in the form of office memoranda. As an example, we have provided a memorandum addressing some of the "office" procedures we used in appendix F. Other general memoranda might explain how to fill out student logs or outline the procedures for checking out documents. As quickly as you can, make your students "feel" that they are in an office environment, not a normal classroom.

Copies of court, legislative, and other agency rules should be distributed and read by the next class. Each student must make a commitment to participate in the course at this first class. And all students should tour the simulation center (or access your course Web page) before the next class.

If you have identified in advance those students who will fill the essential roles, ask them to visit you before the next class. On the basis of this visit, assign essential roles and require the students selected to quickly become familiar with the procedural rules applicable to their positions. You should use these students to help you teach others and to manage the simulation activities.

Begin the second class day by answering questions, and expect a lot of them. If possible, arrange to have recent "alumni" of your simulation course come to class and briefly describe their thoughts and activities during the progression of their course and how the experience benefited them. Their examples will be especially motivating if their course experience helped them acquire their current positions. These alumni should encourage the class to work hard, seek advice, make decisions quickly, and avoid fear of mistakes. You may hope, also, that these former students will invite your students to call or e-mail them with questions.

Describe the setting of the major actions in the simulation and the major roles involved. If time permits, briefly describe the background of some of the major scenarios in the simulation. Last, assign roles to as many people as possible, at least orally. These role assignments should later be committed to writing and distributed to all students.

The leaders of the simulation court, legislature(s), major agencies, and other major groups should meet with their fellow judges, legislative leaders, and partners to get acquainted, review procedural rules, and organize themselves.

Before "Simulation Day 1," distribute scenarios and general information memoranda such as appendixes E–G to your students by placing them in their mailboxes, posting them on your course Web page, or e-mailing them. The third class period starts the simulation and should begin with a conference meeting with the new associates in your simulation office. Create a mood of cooperation with your "associates." It will help if they do not address you as "professor," but instead refer to you by the name you would use in a real office setting. Welcome them to your office, extort them to work hard, and let them get to work. The more enthusiastically you play your role, the easier it will be for the students to fit into theirs.

It is a good idea to select some scenarios that are relatively simple, with activities that can begin quickly and that can be resolved early in the game. This helps all of the students overcome their initial confusion and inertia. Pay special attention as you guide these scenarios and include more detailed taskings in your memoranda. At successive meetings announce to the class the nature of the ongoing actions and display examples of student-generated documents.

Simulation Activity Schedule

Within a very short time the students will be busy in their various roles discussing facts and strategies, filing documents, proposing legislation, and negotiating business deals with other parties. To make everyone aware of these activities and to assist students in their preparation and participation, publish a class-day activity schedule. Use a blackboard in the classroom or in the simulation center or post the schedule to a separate section of a course Web page. Generally, the day's activities should follow the original posted schedule. However, you may set a different schedule to get maximum class participation or for other administrative reasons. Students will quickly learn that they are unable to attend every meeting they should. This is also the case in real practice. They will learn to make alternate arrangements or to compensate for their absence. This published schedule also helps you organize your time to observe as many activities as possible.

Midcourse Correction

Schedule an administrative day sometime before the midpoint of the course. Use this class period to ensure that all of the students are on the right track and moving at an appropriate speed. If some roles or scenarios have not progressed as planned, use this time to bring those involved up to speed by outlining what they *should* have accomplished by this time. If necessary, openly direct students in select roles to accomplish certain tasks; you might even decide to tell them how. For critical scenarios, you can simply declare that certain actions have been completed and decisions made. Instruct those students involved to continue the scenario(s) from that point.

Some students will likely have been reluctant to use one or more of your decision-making forums, such as the simulation court system. Use this time to commend those who have used them and stress to all the need to comply with applicable time requirements. Holding a brief mock trial or other hearing for the class to observe often successfully overcomes this hesitancy. Students will quickly see there is no need to hold back.

This is also a good time to describe for the entire class some of the activities of your simulated community. To give others a sense of what is expected and to reward early efforts, highlight the work of the most active students.

Postsimulation Modifications

Try to spend some time soon after the semester ends to review your extended simulation course. You will have to assess whether your scenarios were too complex, had too many actions going on at the same time, or generated actions you did not anticipate. You will also have to assess whether you assigned appropriate students to important roles. Although no scenario will ever play out the same way twice, you should determine whether they provided the educational benefits you intended. These benefits could include acquiring substantive knowledge, practicing particular skills, or experiencing one of the simulated forums. It is easy to misassign the tasks, usually by giving too many or by giving them in a sequence that does not play out the way you intended. Most novice simulation directors think of every possible task and then assign them in a tightly controlled manner, sequencing and linking as many as possible for all the roles in each scenario. Experience will persuade you to loosen up. Allow your students to discover the goals of their clients and constituents, guiding them, not ordering them, and help them develop their own means of achieving these goals.

Debriefing and Assessment

As we noted in chapter 5, most learning occurs during the debriefing of an education simulation. Determine ahead of time how you plan to conduct the debriefing and how both you and your students should prepare for it. If you required your students to submit logs throughout the simulation, they can review them to prepare a final log discussing what happened and what they learned from the scenarios they were involved with. Decide whether you will require students to prepare written or oral comments. We recommend both.

Written comments force students to bring together their experiences during the simulation. They also must review the documents they were involved with, whether they, another student, or you prepared them. Ask them to first focus their comments on each of the scenarios they were involved with, whatever their role. Have them answer the questions: What was the scenario about? What happened? What did they do and why? How do they assess the effectiveness of their actions and why? What could they have done differently, and what difference do they think alternative actions would have made? Additional questions were outlined in chapter 5.

Ask students who had the role of a decision maker to comment on the cases or issues they were called on to decide. What were the issues? What was their opinion of the presentations of the parties before them? What decision did they come to and why?

Plan for several class days to conduct oral debriefings. Their activity in the simulation will have emotionally charged many students. Begin the oral debriefing with them "as people." Get these emotions out and try to defuse them. Any possible learning during subsequent debriefings of the scenarios will be hampered by students not yet emotionally disengaged from the simulation. A good question to begin with is simply, "How do you feel?"

The next phase of the debriefing should be conducted scenario by scenario, with students who played essential roles making the first comments. There are several reasons for this. Not everyone will be aware of the scenarios they were not a party to. They may not even know all of the activities in their own scenarios. This factual debriefing should focus on the issues in the scenario, the motives and strategies of the parties involved, and their analysis of what took place. During this debriefing many students will experience an "ah hah" moment of understanding, and their experience in the simulation will be imbedded in long-term memory. Start this phase of the debriefing with the question, "What happened?"

You should comment on student activities, strategies, motives, and decisions. You need to compliment students on their successful or correct actions, but you also need to correct their mistakes. Many simulation participants have later commented that their experiences in a simulation course often sent them down appropriate avenues in the professional world. Do not allow students to remain the victims of a negative learning experience. Help them see the value of appropriate alternatives.

During the debriefing it is often helpful to play the "what if" game with several essential roles in the more important scenarios. Even if they made no mistakes, encourage students to consider alternatives they could have taken and to evaluate what effect such actions might have had on the end results. Link what they did during the simulation course to their prior experiences and classes, and help them understand how these classroom simulation experiences will form the basis for their future learning.

Also build into this final debriefing a discussion on how to improve the course. At the very least, ask which documents were erroneous or out of date and what others would be helpful if added. Take notes on these suggested improvements to scenarios and roles.

Assessment of student performance in an extended simulation such as we have described can follow the same principles we discussed in chapter 6 for a simple simulation. In addition, you will have several other measures of performance to consider.

First, you have the written work product of students to assess in the same manner you would a regular writing assignment. The same is true for other student products, such as oral presentations before a simulation body. You will have already seen your students' weekly logs. Taking these logs as a whole, evaluate each student's ability to understand the issues of their scenarios, develop a plan of action, and carry it out.

Much of your students' activities in an extended simulation will be open to subjective assessment on your part. Explain this ahead of time and discuss the basis for your assessment with students individually after the course. For example, you will have to determine whether their behavior was consistent with their authority. Did they demonstrate noteworthy characteristics of organization and leadership? Include in your assessment rubric the various skills built into your course. For example, "communication skills" could be demonstrated by students' proficiency at diplomacy, arguing, interviewing, reporting, note taking, drafting, presenting a case, public speaking, listening, and so forth.

You will discover that extended simulations allow you to develop informed opinions of students' character and abilities, far exceeding what might be discerned in a traditional classroom. These opinions, transferred into recommendations, will be highly sought by your students—particularly the best ones—in applying for employment. The more familiar these potential employers are with your simulation course, the more valuable your recommendations will become.

Final Words of Encouragement

Start small, but with enough students and different scenarios to give everyone a feeling of constant activity on multiple fronts. Do not try to overcontrol and do not get discouraged if students do not see the same issues or ways to solve their tasks that you did.

None of the scenarios will run exactly as you anticipate, and that's OK. Your goal should be to let the students decide what actions to take. If they can reasonably justify a course of action to you as "the senior partner," we recommend letting them take it. If not, direct them to an appropriate path as you normally would as their teacher or as their employer.

Each of our courses started out slowly, and each reached a "critical mass" of activity at different times. When this happens, students begin to think and act like the characters they have been assigned. Although you should resist the temptation to force students to do things exactly as you planned, you can assign a few relatively straightforward activities early in the course to get some momentum going. And always note good student actions to the entire class.

This course consistently generated comments along three themes: I never worked harder in an academic course. I never learned so much. And this was the best educational experience I ever had. And . . . the *students* usually said the same things.

Appendix A

SCENARIO SUMMARY

SCIC/Inglewood v. City of L.A.

Subject Matter: Land Use

California granted Los Angeles Airport (LAX) a noise variance allowing flight operations in excess of the needs of the City of L.A. Many of these flights are over the neighboring City of Inglewood, resulting in 40% of the Inglewood residents living in an excessive noise zone. A group of residents, calling itself the Severely Concerned Inglewood Citizens (SCIC), sued Inglewood alleging the zoning classification of "residential" for their land was now improper, because of the noise. The trial court agreed and stopped the City of Inglewood from issuing any more permits for residential use in the noise area. Inglewood has no space for more residential uses and cannot fill the noise area with other compatible uses, such as industrial. Inglewood citizens will not move away voluntarily. And LAX wants more, not less, flights.

Issues

1. Is noise from an airport a legal "taking" of private property rights by inverse condemnation that would sustain a suit for damages?
2. Can the City of L.A. use its eminent domain powers to expand LAX by condemning land outside its jurisdiction?
3. How can Inglewood citizens who reside outside L.A. restrict flight operations at LAX?
4. How can the City of L.A. increase the number of flights at LAX?

Essential Roles

1. City of Inglewood (mayor, city council, city attorney)
2. LAX (mayor of L.A., director of LAX, L.A. city attorney)
3. State of California (governor, attorney general, legislature)
4. SCIC (any number)

Types of Activity

Political action, trial advocacy, appellate advocacy, negotiation, legislative

Learning Objectives

1. Understand the government power of "taking" private land.
2. Understand a state's power of eminent domain.
3. Practice trial and appellate skills.
4. Develop a political plan to further the interests of the city and a citizen group.
5. Practice negotiation skills.
6. Draft state legislation.

Scenario name used to organize all related documents and roles.

Develop an electronic filing system for all of your documents.

PIRATES LANDING
[C:\Scenario\PiratesLanding\31]

ESSENTIAL ROLES

L.A. COUNTY PLANNING & ZONING DEPT.; HEARING EXAMINER
Represented by:...... Here, one person plays several related roles. .... John HEERN

L.A. COUNTY COUNCIL, MAYOR, COUNTY ATTORNEY
Represented by:................................. Linda FELLEN

GOODWIN CENTURY 21   Peripheral roles; they may be essential roles in other scenarios.
Represented by:........ .... Karl KUZE

Students

INFORMATION COPIES TO:

HUNTINGTON BEACH CITIZENS FOR DUNES PRESERVATION
Represented by:.................................. Amy SMITH

Change this to Inglewood and use the same SCIC group as another scenario.

SIERRA CLUB
Represented by:................................ Dean SACK

DEPARTMENT OF DEFENSE (Army Corps of Engineers)
Represented by:................................ John HERTEL

CALILFORNIA STATE HIGHWAY DEPT.
Represented by:...... Give all roles the same information. .... MaryAnn FISH

This scenario deals with a typical land development issue, with some interesting twists caused by the financial condition of the parties involved and the personalities of the local residents. Local California developer J. W. Goodwin

145

wants to develop 50-some lots out of his half-mile ocean front property along State Highway 1 in Huntington Beach. He is calling his development "Pirates Landing."

You know developers . . . their quest for monetary profit is the motivating force whether they be fast-buck operators or conscientious and responsible business persons engaged in converting raw land into attractive places to settle and/or to invest in. After all, that's what the capitalistic system is built on. Everyone in this scenario is a part of this process, and so that we can reflect the correlative desire to improve Southern California.

Give some guidance on "how" the student should play the role.

For you L.A. county officials, who are unsung, overworked, underpaid, and inexperienced with respect to coping with some elements of a development deal like the one here, try to extract the best out of any proposal, to screen out the worst, and to help the dreams of our residents to attain some degree of financial reward and yet preserve the environment that made our community so attractive in the first place.

Goodwin (played by Karl Kuze wearing the hats of the California developer and of his attorney) seems to be among the better developers with his willingness to discuss his project in a responsible manner. He wants to make money on this deal, but he is equally interested in establishing a solid foothold in the area for future, and greater, rewards.

We will be working with the actual documents from the real Pirates Landing rezoning application (which was actually built in St. Augustine, Florida), including the plat map submitted, pertinent newspaper clippings from the *St. Augustine Record* to provide some local flavor, a copy of the local ordinances, the County Comprehensive Plan, and some application

Point students to relevant documents.

We have, among our L.A. County documents, the "density credits" regulations referenced in the application papers. This document should be a part of your role file package. The density credit element appears as an amendment to the zoning ordinance. We have beautiful "blown-up" colored renderings of the proposed project plat, drawn by Damaso Saavedra during last semester's simulation course, which Goodwin should use in his presentation before the Zoning Board. Those responsible should schedule that hearing as soon as he requests it (you may even unofficially prod him to do so). In the past, we sometimes have been able to arrange for Mr. Martin Klauber, Esq., one of our local hearing examiners, to sit with students and chair this hearing, and we will try to arrange a suitable time for him *Outside expert* emester as well. We videotaped the hearings Mr. Klauber chaired in previous semesters. His participation has been considered by all involved to be an invaluable experience, and the cumulative learning available from the tapes has helped each succeeding simulation to increase the professionalism and sophistication of presentation. I urge you to view at least some of each before your hearing. The University Media Center will arrange for you to see these tapes. (The previous hearings ran about 3 hours.) If you want to videotape your hearing, let me know.

When you have problems, don't hesitate to consult with me. I won't have all the answers you need, but we'll do our best.

Enough to tell this group how to act.

The Huntington Beach Citizens who fight any change in the county will be very vocal on this, as they are for any proposed change. Expect the Sierra Club to get into the act, as any development affecting the salt marsh lying between the ocean and State Highway 1 should concern them, as should the information contained in the publication by the Duke University Press, entitled "Living with the East Florida Shore," senior editors Orrin H. Pilkey, Jr., and William J. Neal (1984). A copy of this article is at document file #262 for your use. The Army Corps of Engineers may be interested, if any section 404 wetlands matters are involved.

Appendix C
SELECTIVE AND SEQUENCED SCENARIO

SCIC/Inglewood v. City of Los Angeles

This guide contains all of the scenario components.
Scenario Guide

SUMMARY: The City of Inglewood zoned a land area residential, even though it is in a high noise zone caused by aircraft departures from LAX. The homeowners in this area want to stop the noise, to be relocated, or to receive damages. There is also a question of whether the zoning is legal. LAX wants to increase operations.

PROCESS: Trial Litigation, Appellate Litigation, Negotiation, Administrative, Political

ROLES	STUDENT
*City of Inglewood (Mayor)	_____
*SCIC	_____
*LAX (L.A. City Attorney)	_____
*California Governor	_____
CALTRANS	_____
FAA	_____
(*Essential role)	

Documents

Documents are kept in sequentially numbered folders. Ensure they are there before each simulation.

SCIC v. City of Inglewood, appellate decision (2641)
Articles: Effects of jet noise on mortality rates (1248, 1990)
Articles: Effects of noise on health (1656, 1671, 1704, 1992)
Sample legal complaint (*SCIC v. L.A.*) (2001, 2007)
Sample claim for damages against LAX (2008)
Graph of jet noise levels (2139)
Newspaper articles: (1662, 1675, 2753)

Direct some students to some articles; put other articles in your simulation newspaper.

ROLE INTERESTS

City of Inglewood	Support residents; reduce flights at LAX, or at least stop expansion
SCIC	Reduce airplane operations at LAX; sue for damages
LAX	Get increased flight operations
FAA	Safety and airline business concerns
California	Develop a political solution

Quick reminder of general goals for each role.

SCIC/Inglewood v. City of Los Angeles

Plan

> The plan contains the information, documents, and tasks for each role in the scenario, separated by the simulation (class) day when they will be given to the student in the role.

Role: **SCIC**

Day 1

> Role background information, interests, and direction to certain documents, and suggested actions to consider or to be on the alert for from other roles.

INFORMATION

SCIC represents r s in Inglewood, California, whose property rests with tour.

This role may provide you with an opportunity to show your skills as a constitutional scholar. You might sow seeds which, properly nurtured and harvested, could let you reap the overturning of the famous airport noise case of *Griggs v. Allegheny County.* You will begin with the (fictitious) class action case of *SCIC v. City of Inglewood,* decided by Student Judge Jon Fleuchaus in a previous simulation. This decision is document #2641 in the document file.

The *SCIC v. Inglewood* case raised the issue of whether the City of Inglewood could properly maintain zoning that classified plaintiffs' neighborhood as a residential, single-family detached housing district, even though it lay directly beneath the flight path of commercial airliners passing overhead at altitudes of less than 500 feet to take off and land on the north runway at LAX, slightly less that 2 miles to the west.

Holding that the zoning had been appropriate when it was first established (before 1959, when the first jet aircraft landed at LAX), Judge Fleuchaus found that plaintiffs were exposed to intermittent sound levels as high as 116 PNdB (perceived noise level), whereas the State of California Department of Transportation (CALTRANS) has set 78 PNdB as the highest level permissible for protection from noise-induced injury. Judge Fleuchaus also found that exposure to noise at the volumes within the 30 NEF noise contour (a scale used by zoning officials to separate uses of land) is harmful to hearing and causes stress-related diseases, and that more than one half of the residents in Inglewood live in areas within noise contours exceeding 30 NEF. Some of this evidence can be seen in documents 1248, 1990, and 1992 in the document file.

> Direction to look at documents.

Dr. William Meecham, Department of Engineering, UCLA, testified that tests had determined that the overwhelmingly dominant source of the noise in Inglewood is the operations at LAX and that the death rate in neighborhoods directly under the LAX landing pattern and within 3 miles of the airport was 19% higher than among residents 6 miles from the airport. You can see some of this evidence in documents1990 and 2139.

Judge Fleuchaus held that plaintiffs were subjected to substantial exposure to damaging levels of noise attributable to airport operations at LAX, which constituted a change of conditions, and the existing zoning could no longer be maintained under state constitutional police powers. He said that the fact that Inglewood had no control over the imposition of the objectionable levels of noise did not relieve Inglewood of its duty to exercise its zoning power to benefit public health, safety, and general welfare. He finally held that Inglewood could not maintain the existing residential-class zoning of plaintiffs' properties.

Inglewood, a low to moderate income "bedroom community," cannot rezone more than 20% of the residential property in its jurisdiction and relocate residents within other areas of the city that are not severely noise impacted because there is not enough qualifying land in Inglewood to accommodate them all.

To rezone the noise-impacted area to uses that are not noise sensitive is not a solution because the existing residential properties could still legally remain as "nonconforming" for decades. Additionally, Inglewood could not reasonably fill all of this land with industrial uses.

TASKS

> Give specific guidance to students. This gets action going.

a. Move as quickly as possible to file suit against LAX, the City of L.A., or both. Discuss this with the City of Inglewood and decide whether to sue jointly.
b. Prepare a memorandum on your objectives and legal theories.

Day 3

> You must plan how much information to give to each role—and when.

> Specific writing project.

INFORMATION

CALTRANS has issued an annual "variance" authorizing LAX to operate at higher noise levels than are permitted by state statute. In spite of this, the state permitted LAX to execute a major construction program to further expand the existing level of operations at LAX. Assessing the U.S. Supreme Court decision in *PRDC v. Electrical Union,* you do not expect to be permitted to enjoin that construction; however, you do believe that you should be allowed to enjoin any increase in flight operations that increases the noise levels imposed on Inglewood.

TASKS

> VERY specific direction of what you want, and when.

c. Submit a brief with Log #3 on the following issues:
   1) In operating LAX at levels of service that exceed its own needs, is Los Angeles either operating its airport to that extent in an *ultra vires* manner, or is it operating it as an implied agent of the State of California? What can we do to get CALTRANS into the suit?
   2) Is the state's use of LAX a violation of the charter of government that it granted to Inglewood?

3) Is the state effecting a "taking" of the property and the rights of self-government constitutionally protected to the property owners of Inglewood?

4) Do we have a possible action on inverse condemnation against LAX?

Day 5

These tasks are graded like any homework.

Instructors and students must keep track of both real time and simulation time.

TASKS

d. Initiate a complaint by next week (real time) against L.A. Seek to enjoin the activities that cause the damages; however, look at all possible causes of action.

e. What claim for damages do you have? Against the both?

Direct them to roles in other scenarios with related tasks.

f. Talk to the attorney for NIHOLA. See if we can pool achieve common goals.

g. Continue to put pressure on legislators at all levels. This may be our ultimate solution.

Day 8

Suggest ideas related to course topics.

Keep them thinking of alternative solutions.

TASKS

h. Is there a possible damages theory you can pursue on the basis of "latent defect," because at the time of the current zoning and construction of LAX no one could anticipate the technology of jet aircraft, which produce the noise complained of here?

i. Is there a legal or practical problem created by L.A.'s offer of money generated by LAX to Inglewood to lessen the impact of the noise from LAX on Inglewood's citizens?

Day 11

Follow up on a previous Task (i).

Be sure to give these facts to other roles.

TASKS

j. Back to the issue of L.A.'s offering money from its LAX operations to Inglewood—is it a proper function of the City of Inglewood to accept the money? Is there an equal protection or due process issue here?

Role: **City of Inglewood**

Day 1

INFORMATION

[Provide the City of Inglewood with the same information provided to SCIC.]

TASKS

a. You will have to move as quickly as possible to file suit against LAX, L.A., or both. What will be your objectives and legal theories?

Day 3

> A tip, in case the student did not pick it up on Day 1 or 2.

INFORMATION

Faced with this decision by Judge Fleuchaus, you have now concluded that your only recourse is to bring suit against the City of L.A. seeking injunctive relief to force L.A. to reduce the level of operations at LAX to the point where they no longer exceed the needs of L.A. itself.

> SCIC was told to do this on Day 1; this is a check to ensure these parties talk.

TASKS

b. Discuss possible theories of suit with SCIC and assist with preparation of the SCIC legal brief. If you have any interests distinct from SCIC identify them in your next log.

Day 5

> Ultimately you get them to your learning objective.

TASKS

c. Initiate suit as soon as possible against the City of L.A., basing it on inverse condemnation.

Day 8

> Here is an example of how you can modify scenarios. The actual case dealt with expanding LAX for the 1984 Olympics.

INFORMATION

The goal of the planned LAX $200 million expansion program is to greatly enlarge the airport capacity to accommodate ground traffic by double-decking the interior access and egress roadways) and by adding terminal space. LAX has publicly stated that it can now expand air operations from 36 million to 46 million passengers per year.

Recently, LAX offered to provide the City of Inglewood with several million dollars per year to use to buy out houses underneath the approach paths to LAX. The money would come from profits in the operation of LAX. If you accept, however, you can only offer to make purchases; you cannot compel homeowners to move. What would the basis of the purchase price be?

> Tasks can be as focused as any exam questions.

TASKS

d. Do you see any legal problems arising from this offer of money to your city to use to lessen the adverse impact of the noise on your citizens?

e. Although L.A. may have the right to operate an airport, is its decision of the "level of operations" a proprietary right? If so, can a case be made that such a right cannot be superior to Inglewood's essential powers rights guaranteed by the state constitution, legislation, and its charter?

f. Is there a difference in the legal effect of the City of L.A.'s eminent domain power beyond its boundary as opposed to within it? Is this power with the city or the airport?

g. Do you have a cause of action because L.A. has "taken" the constitutional right of your citizens to self-government?

Role: **LAX (City Attorney)**

Day 1

INFORMATION

> This provides background on this role and a "heads-up" on concerns of another role.

[Provide the L.A. city attorney for LAX with the same information on Day 1 provided to SCIC, but with the following additional information.]

The goal of the recent LAX $200 million expansion was to enlarge the airport ground traffic capacity by double-decking the access and egress roadways and by adding considerable terminal space. With the added ground capacity, LAX has publicly stated that it will now expand air operations from 36 million to 46 million passengers per year.

This news has upset an organized group of residents of nearby Inglewood, who recently received the appellate decision of their suit against the City of Inglewood because of the noise from overflying aircraft.

Recently, LAX offered to provide Inglewood with several million dollars per year to use for buying out houses underneath the approach paths to LAX. But Inglewood, if it accepts, can only offer to make such purchases. It cannot compel acceptance, however.

TASKS

> Action taken on each task is reported in the student's log.

a. Read the *SCIC v. Inglewood* case (Document # 2641) to get an idea of why the citizens of Inglewood are so upset. Then find out all you can about their problems.

b. Your goal is to continue to operate at the current level of operations, and you want to expand.

c. Determine the state authority that allows you to operate LAX. Look first in the California Government Code and the Public Utilities Code.

Day 5

TASKS

> Specific tasks can be graded like an exam or a practical exercise, but the students are more likely to view them as "work from their boss."

d. Does the City of L.A., LAX, or both have the power of eminent domain? How, if at all, does this eminent domain power play in this scenario?
e. What is your authority for operating LAX at levels of service that exceed the needs of Los Angeles? Look to the state (CALTRANS) for the answer.
f. Is the state liable for any damages? On what basis?

> Keep nudging the parties together.

Day 8

INFORMATION

> If the student hasn't picked it up, guide him or her in the correct direction.

Consider, as one tact in defending against the petition to enjoin you from "excessive operational levels," the position that as a charter home rule city L.A. can govern itself within its powers without interference by the state or by the City of Inglewood.

TASKS

g. Is there any prohibition against LAX's "taking" land in Inglewood? Do the flights from LAX violate Inglewood's zoning ordinance?
h. What is your legal basis for giving money generated by LAX to Inglewood to buy land with?
i. Is there a way to get the FAA in as the defendant in any suit against you? Is federal preemption an issue here?

Role: **CALTRANS**

Day 6

INFORMATION

> It is hoped this role has been contacted by the L.A. city attorney. If not, this will prod him.

Most of what you need to know about the facts of this scenario you can get from the L.A. city attorney for LAX. An additional fact is that for the past several years CALTRANS has granted LAX variances from the noise level restrictions that would have limited its airport operations.

TASKS

a. Study your authority to regulate the operations of LAX. Look at the California Public Utilities Code and the California Administrative Code.

SCIC/Inglewood v. L.A.

Tasks

Role: **SCIC**

We only include here the taskings for the SCIC role.

This is your "scorecard"; use it to ensure all actions are being accomplished. It's also a good resource for assigning grades.

TASK	DONE	COMMENTS
Day 1		
a. Move as quickly as possible to file suit against LAX, the City of L.A., or both Discuss this with the City of Inglewood and decide whether to sue jointly.	Day 2 \n\n Day 7	Reported on discussion with Inglewood officials \n\n Filed suit on "taking" theory
b. Prepare a memorandum on your objectives and legal theories	Day 3	Good memo (A–)
Day 3		
c. Submit a brief with Log #3 on the following issues: \n 1) In operating LAX at levels of service that exceed its own needs, is Los Angeles either operating its airport to that extent in an ultra vires manner, or is it operating it as an implied agent of the State of California? What can we do to get CALTRANS into the suit? \n 2) Is the state's use of LAX a violation of the charter of government that it granted to Inglewood? \n 3) Is the state effecting a "taking" of the property and the rights of self-government constitutionally protected to the property owners of Inglewood? \n 4) Do we have a possible action on inverse condemnation against LAX?	Day 6	Good brief (B+), but focused too much on the "taking" issue, and only briefly discussed inverse condemnation

Your comments here can discuss the substance of what the student produced or the mechanics (he or she got it done) or both. Use this for grading.

(continued)

TASK	DONE	COMMENTS
Day 5		
d. Initiate a complaint by next week (real time) against L.A. Seek to enjoin the activities that cause the damages; however, look at all possible causes of action.	Day 7	Joined with City of Inglewood (Inglewood did most of the work on the complaint)
e. What claim for damages do you have? Against the city, the state, or both?		
f. Talk to the attorney for NIHOLA. See if we can pool our resources to achieve common goals.	Day 7	Reported discussion with NIHOLA attorney; good report
g. Continue to put pressure on legislators at all levels. This may be our ultimate solution.		
Day 8		
h. Is there a possible damages theory you can pursue on the basis of "latent defect," because at the time of the current zoning and construction of LAX no one could anticipate the technology of jet aircraft, which produce the noise complained of here?		The tasks are cut and pasted from the scenario plan.
i. Is there a legal or practical problem created by L.A.'s offer of money generated by LAX to Inglewood to lessen the impact of the noise from LAX on Inglewood's citizens?		
Day 11		
j. Back to the issue of L.A.'s offering money from its LAX operations to Inglewood—is it a proper function of the City of Inglewood to accept the money? Is there an equal protection or due process issue here?		

SIMULATION OFFICE
WASHINGTON, D.C.

These memoranda are prepared in advance. This is how students get information and tasks.

Simulation 33
Day 1

MEMORANDUM FOR SCIC

Subject: SCIC/Inglewood

INFORMATION

Cut and paste this from the scenario plan.

You or your assistant can keep these memos in a folder, by simulation day, and give them to students on the day they should get the information and tasks.

SCIC represents residential property owners in Inglewood, California, whose property rests within the 30 NEF noise contour.

This role may provide you with an opportunity to show your skills as a constitutional scholar. You might sow seeds which, properly nurtured and harvested, could let you reap the overturning of the famous airport noise case of *Griggs v. Allegheny County.* You will begin with the (fictitious) class action case of *SCIC v. City of Inglewood,* decided by Student Judge Jon Fleuchaus in a previous simulation. This decision is document #2641 in the document file.

Direct students to specific documents.

The *SCIC v. Inglewood* case raised the issue of whether the City of Inglewood could properly maintain zoning that classified plaintiffs' neighborhood as a residential, single-family detached housing district, even though it lay directly beneath the flight path of commercial airliners passing overhead at altitudes of less than 500 feet to take off and land on the north runway at LAX, slightly less that 2 miles to the west.

Holding that the zoning had been appropriate when it was first established (before 1959, when the first jet aircraft landed at LAX), Judge Fleuchaus found that plaintiffs were exposed to intermittent sound levels as high as 116 PNdB, whereas the CALTRANS has set 78 PNdB as the highest level permissible for protection from noise-induced injury. Judge Fleuchaus also found that exposure to noise at the volumes within the 30 NEF noise contour (a scale used by zoning officials to separate uses of land) is harmful to hearing and causes stress-related diseases, and that more than one half of the residents in Inglewood live in areas within noise contours exceeding 30 NEF. Some of this evidence can be seen in documents 1248, 1990, and 1992 in the document file.

Dr. William Meecham, Department of Engineering, UCLA, testified that tests had determined that the overwhelmingly dominant source of the noise in Inglewood is the operations at LAX and that the death rate in neighborhoods directly under the LAX landing pattern and within 3 miles of the airport was 19% higher than among residents 6 miles from the airport. You can see some of this evidence in documents1990 and 2139.

Judge Fleuchaus held that plaintiffs were subjected to substantial exposure to damaging levels of noise attributable to airport operations at LAX, which constituted a change of conditions, and the existing zoning could no longer be maintained under state constitutional police powers. He said that the fact that Inglewood had no control over the imposition of the objectionable levels of noise did not relieve Inglewood of its duty to exercise its zoning power to benefit public health, safety, and general welfare. He finally held that Inglewood could not maintain the existing residential-class zoning of plaintiffs' properties.

Inglewood, a low to moderate income "bedroom community," cannot rezone more than 20% of the residential property in its jurisdiction and relocate residents within other areas of the city that are not severely noise impacted because there is not enough qualifying land in Inglewood to accommodate them all.

To rezone the noise-impacted area to uses that are not noise sensitive is not a solution because the existing residential properties could still legally remain as "nonconforming" for decades. Additionally, Inglewood could not reasonably fill all of this land with industrial uses.

TASKS Again taken from the scenario plan.

 a. Move as quickly as possible to file suit against LAX, the City of L.A., or both. Discuss this with the City of Inglewood and decide whether to sue jointly.
 b. Prepare a memorandum on your objectives and legal theories.

/s/
The Partners

SIMULATION OFFICE
WASHINGTON, D.C.

Simulation 33
Day 3

MEMORANDUM FOR SCIC

Just cut and paste from your master file to distribute information and assign new tasks on the day you want.

Subject: SCIC/Inglewood

INFORMATION

CALTRANS has issued an annual "variance" authorizing LAX to operate at higher noise levels than are permitted by state statute. In spite of this, the state permitted LAX to execute a major construction program to further expand the existing level of operations at LAX. Assessing the U.S. Supreme Court decision in *PRDC v. Electrical Union,* you do not expect to be permitted to enjoin that construction; however, you do believe that you should be allowed to enjoin any increase in flight operations that increases the noise levels imposed on Inglewood.

Keep the same task number as on your scenario plan.

TASKS

c. Submit a brief with Log #3 on the following issues:
   1) In operating LAX at levels of service that exceed its own needs, is Los Angeles either operating its airport to that extent in an *ultra vires* manner, or is it operating it as an implied agent of the State of California? What can we do to get CALTRANS into the suit?
   2) Is the state's use of LAX a violation of the charter of government that it granted to Inglewood?
   3) Is the state effecting a "taking" of the property and the rights of self-government constitutionally protected to the property owners of Inglewood?
   4) Do we have a possible action on inverse condemnation against LAX?

/s/
The Partners

Appendix D
THE SIMULATION NEWS

The Simulation News

Vol. XXXIII [Semester]

Publisher: Professor Jim Brown

Editor: John Hertel

Investigative Reporters: The Entire Class

No. 3 [Issue]

Simulation Time: _____   Real Time: _____

[Keep track of "both" times.]

MAYOR WANTS NOISE CRACKDOWN

City of Inglewood Mayor, Joe Welling, announced that he would meet with state legislators later this month to discuss new legislation aimed at reducing aircraft noise at lax. "If the airlines will not police themselves, and we can't get help from the FAA, then this state will control its own destiny," said Mayor Welling.

[Report simulation events or suggest new action.]

PRESS RELEASE
Sept. 10, 20xx (RT)

The FAA announced today it would fund a study of aircraft noise surrounding LAX. The contract for the study is expected to be awarded within 90 days, and could cost as much as $800,000.

HIGHWAY DEPT. CONDUCTS HEARING
ON REALIGNMENT OF HIGHWAY 1
DEVELOPER MEETS WITH PROBLEMS IN PIRATES LANDING PROJECT

Notice to all "roles."   By Susan Smith

Huntington Beach, Sept 8, 20xx—(RT) The State Highway Department held a public hearing today to consider a proposed change in State Highway 1 along Huntington Beach. The proposal presented by Goodwin Century 21 would realign the highway to include an S-shape curve along a half-mile stretch of the road. The proposed realignment will allow for the construction of a 400-unit condominium development on 70-acre beachfront property currently owned by J. W. Goodwin. Earlier this year, Goodwin had been the target of a state corruption probe investigating allegations of bribery of county zoning officials.

At the hearing, the Highway Department heard testimony from the developer as well as representatives of Los Angeles County, the Army Corps of Engineers, citizens groups, and private citizens. A spokesman for the county voiced concerns regarding the proposed curvature of the highway and its impact on the safety of automobile operators and pedestrians. A representative of the Sierra Club voiced opposition to the plan because of the potential danger to beach dunes, wetlands, and endangered species in the construction area. A lone elderly citizen, who identified himself as a retired college professor interested in purchasing one of the new condos, was the only supporter of the proposal to speak at the hearing.

Administrative Notes (From the "Administrator") — Guidance to "students."

1. I have noticed that several students have not followed the required format in completing your logs. Please refer to the LOGS memorandum, Day 0.
2. Please attach to your logs a copy of all material you produce in your role. If it is a large document, map, etc., just describe it and tell me where it is.
3. Please keep the simulation center CLEAN! The maintenance personnel have complained to the assistant dean about spilled drinks and food (especially pizza) in and around the room. There can be NO food or drinks in the library!
4. YES, the students assigned as judges DO have the authority to issue standard orders from the bench. If it is an appealable order, you are free to appeal. If it is not, you may have to live with it. If you think it is an abuse of power (as a judge or as a student), bring it up with me.

"How the state searches for solutions to aircraft noise."

Here's the reason you have a noise problem; your roofing material is 0.014 inches too thin.

Outlet for student/role creativity.

Appendix E
SIMULATION OFFICE
MEMORANDUM: LOGS

Simulation Office
Washington, D.C.

Simulation 33
Day 0

Memorandum for New Associates

Subject: Logs

Your are required to submit a log of your course activities once a week—on Thursday. These logs are our primary means of analyzing how specific scenarios and the simulation in general are developing. They are also our primary source of information concerning your abilities, efforts, and work product, upon which we will determine whether to offer you a partnership (A), keep you on as an associate (B) or a clerk (C), or suggest you look for employment elsewhere (D or F). Use the log format below.

Include in your logs all of your efforts on behalf of our clients, such as notes of meetings and discussions you have with anyone related to the simulation. Include responses to specific tasks assigned by a senior partner, noting the task number where appropriate. Also, include your thoughts on how the scenario is developing, plans for your future action, suggestions for improving the scenario, and any problems you encounter.

Attach a copy of all original work you produce to your logs. This includes everything from a court pleading to an article or cartoon for *The Simulation News.* Be certain to put your name and corresponding log number on each work product. If the document was the result of a joint effort, identify your contribution.

/s/
The Senior Partners

(Sample Format for Logs)

Name: Simulation 33
Role: Log # _____
Scenario: (Date)

Summary of activities, responses to taskings (by number), plans for future
actions, problems, and thoughts about the scenario. Describe and attach any
documents produced for this scenario.

Role:
Scenario:

Appendix F

SIMULATION OFFICE MEMORANDUM: GENERAL OFFICE PROCEDURES

Simulation Office
Washington, D.C.

Simulation 33
Day 0

This memo was for a law school simulation course.

Memorandum for New Associates

Subject: General Office Procedures

Welcome to the Simulation Law Offices. You are to be congratulated on your selection of our office as a means to learn about land use and development issues in a hands-on environment. We have every confidence that we will exceed your expectations. Your education will not come cheap, however. The pace of your learning through this simulation course will always be fast, and at times it will seem impossible. This course is not for the lazy or for those unable to make quick and accurate decisions. You are expected to dedicate yourself to this course for the next 4 months. To succeed, you will have to.

This memorandum contains instructions and information concerning our simulation course. Read them at once and understand them completely. If you have any questions, ask. It is hard to play "catch up" in this course.

You will be graded in much the same way as we would decide whether to keep you in our "office." If you do not actively participate in your scenarios, complete the assigned tasks, or otherwise fail to contribute to the course, you will be asked to leave the office (D or F). If you accomplish the bare minimum of all assigned tasks you will be allowed to stay on as a clerk (C). Those of you who bring zealous representation to our clients and their interests and who demonstrate your knowledge of and skill with the rules of the judicial, administrative, and legislative forums in which you will practice and who outmaneuver, outlitigate, or outnegotiate your adversaries will be offered to stay on a partnership track (B). Immediate partnership (A) will be offered to those of you who show mastery of the issues, procedures, and lawyering skills involved in this course.

Once you receive your role assignments you are on your own. Most of you will also receive one or more office memoranda for at least one of your roles giving you some background information, resource materials to review, and general or specific guidance on how to proceed with your role. Get started with your role at once. You will be able to make corrections to your activities later, but waiting too long to get started may mean the loss of our client.

Those of you who do not receive instructions on how to proceed with your role(s) should be prepared to move to action when prompted by another party or whenever you sense a need to represent your client's interests (most often from reading *The Simulation News*). If your role is a real public or private organization, become familiar with it.

In some roles you will simulate both the attorney and the client. In a few you will simulate a non-lawyer role. The scenario memorandum should make this clear. If you are assigned an institutional role (FAA, mayor of L.A., EPA, etc.) you will be required to act for all offices and officials subordinate to this role not assigned to another student. Furthermore, you will be required to provide information to other students seeking information relevant to your role. For example, whoever is assigned to be the Army Corps of Engineers must be able to explain its wetlands permit requirements to anyone who inquires.

The official start of this simulation is Monday, August 28, 20XX. This will be "Day 1" of the simulation. Also, note on your course calendar that each real week is equivalent to four months of simulation time. The simulation time begins on January 1, 20XX–2. You may only cite a court case or use passed legislation after its effective date.

You may solicit advice and direction from a "senior partner." We will post the times and places we can be reached. However, this is a course where you learn by doing, even if the "doing" is wrong. We expect and, to an extent, encourage mistakes. Make them now, not after you graduate. You are also encouraged to obtain whatever expert advice you can from any source you choose. In fact, we have a list of some people in public and private practice who have shown a willingness over the past to assist students in this course. We only ask that you be considerate in soliciting their advice and that you report these activities in your logs.

You are expected to be present in class each day of the semester. Check your mailbox (or e-mail) before coming to class. We will assign seats for all students, attempting to seat related roles together. Each class will begin with administrative remarks, followed by "official" announcements and late-breaking "news flashes." Previously scheduled legislative sessions will come next, followed by scheduled activities requiring the entire class. These activities may take anywhere from 5 minutes to an hour. At their conclusion you are free to attend scheduled activities or otherwise go about your business.

Activities are scheduled either by mutual agreement of the affected parties or by listing them on the blackboard in the classroom (or on the course Web page) before the start of class. Please give as much advance notice of these meetings as possible and make every effort to schedule them during or immediately after a class period.

Again, welcome to the office. More than any other time during your school career, the maxim "you get out of it what you put into it" applies to this simulation course. We look forward to a productive relationship.

/s/
The Partners

Appendix G

SIMULATION OFFICE MEMORANDUM: SIMULATION CENTER

Simulation Office
Washington, D.C.

Simulation 33
Day 0

Memorandum for New Associates

Subject: Simulation Center

Room 4L-222 will be our Simulation Center. This room contains much of what you will need to participate in this simulation course. It and the assigned classroom are the physical focal points of the course. Each can become one of several forums, depending on the needs of the scenarios and roles you will simulate. The Simulation Center contains the following:

Student Mailboxes: These mail slots are located on your right as you enter the room. Each student will be assigned a slot, with his/her name beneath it. These "mailboxes" are used for all forms of communication: service of legal papers, announcements of hearings or meetings, new scenario information, memoranda from a "senior partner," personal notes from friends, etc. There are two rules regarding these mailboxes:

> Rule 1: Check your mailbox each weekday;
> Rule 2: Do not look at/remove anything from another's mailbox without permission.

Documents File: Much of the essential resource materials you need to fulfill your roles in this simulation course are contained in the Document File. These documents are stored in the file cabinets next to the Simulation Court Files and contain documents of all sorts, from actual newspaper articles of people or events related to our scenarios to fictitious background material and from actual court pleadings to the work product of previous students. Each of these documents is in a sequentially numbered file folder.

During the course, you may be directed to specific documents by your scenario memoranda, a "senior partner," or another student. Not all students are given the same guidance. In addition, you are encouraged to search for and use any other documents you believe will benefit your clients or your cause.

Some of the folders in the Documents File contain only a single copy of the document; some contain several copies. If you remove one of several copies, you must complete a "Check Out" slip (located on top of the cabinet) and place it in the document folder. You may remove the single/last copy of a document from the folder only to read it in the Simulation Center or to copy it. If the document you need is missing, notify our research assistant or a senior partner.

Court Files: The Simulation Court Files consist of the top two drawers of the file cabinet immediately to the left as you enter the Simulation Center and a box on top of the cabinet. Instructions on how to use the Simulation Court Files are contained in your Simulation Court Rules.

Legislative Files: The top drawer of the file cabinet under the Simulation Center Mailboxes contains blank forms, legislative rules, and copies of pending and approved Simulation legislation you will need to succeed in your legislative roles. If you have any questions concerning legislative activities, discuss them with the students assigned to legislative leadership roles.

The Simulation News: This is our course newspaper. Each of you has the additional role assignments of ace reporter, editor, and associate publisher. You may write and publish any article you deem necessary to the course. Some of you will be *directed* to submit articles for the newspaper.

This paper will also serve as our means of legal notice for all public meetings and administrative hearings. To a limited extent it will report court activities. However, you must follow specific court procedural rules concerning service of process and notice requirements.

Please deposit all submissions for the paper in the folder next to the mailboxes in the Simulation Center. All articles must be "camera ready" on an 8 1/2″ × 11″ sheet of white paper. Write your name on the back of the paper. If you want to publish a document that is longer than five pages, prepare a brief summary of the document for inclusion in *The Simulation News* and attach it to the document. We will make two copies of the document and put them in a special binder in the Simulation Center and publish your summary.

The newspaper will be published every Thursday. Articles submitted by the end of class on Wednesday will be published in the Thursday edition.

Please keep the Simulation Center as neat as possible.

/s/
The Senior Partners

Chapter 1

Astin, A. W. (1993). *What matters in college: Four critical years revisited.* San Francisco: Jossey-Bass.

Bransford, J. D., Brown, A. L., & Cocking, R. R. (Eds.). (2000). *How people learn: Brain, mind, experience, and school.* Commission on Behavioral and Social Sciences and Education National Research Council. Washington, DC: National Academy Press.

Brookfield, S. D. (1991). *The skillful teacher: On technique, trust, and responsiveness in the classroom.* San Francisco: Jossey-Bass.

Burns, A. C., & Gentry, J. W. (1998). Motivating students to engage in experiential learning: A tension-to-learn theory. *Simulation & Gaming, 29,* 133–151.

Cunningham, J. B. (1984). Assumptions underlying the use of different types of simulations. *Simulation & Games, 15,* 213–234.

Deep learning, surface learning. (1993). *AAHE Bulletin, 45*(8), 14–17.

Dentler, D. (1994). Cooperative learning and American history. *Cooperative Learning and College Teaching,4*(3), 9–12.

Duffy, D. K., & Jones, J. W. (1995). *Teaching within the rhythms of the semester.* San Francisco: Jossey-Bass.

Finkel, D. L. (2000). *Teaching with your mouth shut.* Portsmouth, NH: Boyton/Cook Publishers.

Gabennesch, H. (1992). The enriched syllabus: To convey a larger vision. *The National Teaching and Learning Forum, 1*(4), 4.

Gaff, J. G. (1992). Beyond politics: The educational issues inherent in multicultural education. *Change: The Magazine of Higher Learning, 24*(1), 31–35.

Gibbs, G. I. (1978). *Dictionary of gaming, modeling and simulations.* Beverly Hills, CA: Sage.

Giezkowski, W. (1992). The influx of older students can revitalize college teaching. *The Chronicle of Higher Education, 38*(29), 133–134.

Gosen, J., & Washbush, J. (1999). As teachers and researchers, where do we go from here? *Simulation & Gaming, 30,* 292–303.

Greenblat, C. S. (1981). Seeing forests and trees: Gaming-simulation and contemporary problems of learning and communication. In C. S. Greenblat & R. D. Duke (Eds.), *Principles and practices of gaming simulation* (pp. 13–18). Beverly Hills, CA: Sage.

Jones, K. (1987). *Simulations: A handbook for teachers and trainers.* London: Kogan Page.

Leamnson, R. (1999). *Thinking about teaching and learning: Developing habits of learning with first year college and university students.* Sterling, VA: Stylus Press.

Nelson, C. E. (1996). Student diversity requires different approaches to college teaching, even in math and science. *American Behavioral Scientist, 40*(2), 165–175.

Orbach, E. (1979). Simulation games and motivation for learning: A theoretical framework. *Simulation & Games, 10,* 3–40.

Petranek, C., Corey, F., & Black, R. (1992). Three levels of learning in simulations: Participating, debriefing, and journal writing. *Simulation & Gaming, 23,* 174–185.

Rhem, J. (1995a). Deep/surface approaches to learning: An introduction. *The National Teaching & Learning Forum, 5*(1), 1–3.

Rhem, J. (1995b). Close-up: Going deep. *The National Teaching & Learning Forum, 5*(1), 4.

Simpson, E. L. (1980). Adult learning theory: A state of the art. In H. Lasker, J. Moore, & E. L. Simpson (Eds.), *Adult development and approaches to learning.* Washington, DC: National Institute of Education.

Theall, M., & Franklin, J. (1999). What have we learned? A synthesis and some guidelines for effective motivation in higher education. In M. Theall (Ed.), *Motivation from within: Approaches for encouraging faculty and students to succeed* (pp. 99–109). New Directions for Teaching and Learning, no. 78. San Francisco: Jossey-Bass.

Woods, D. R. (1996). *Instructor's guide for problem-based learning: How to gain the most from PBL* (3rd ed.). Retrieved January 14, 1997, from http://chemeng.mcmaster.ca/pbl/pbl.htm [URL verified October 23, 2001.]

Chapter 2

Birnbaum, R. (1982). Games and simulations in higher education. *Simulation & Games, 13,* 3–11.

Finkel, D. L. (2000). *Teaching with your mouth shut.* Portsmouth, NH: Boyton/Cook.

Gibbs, G. I. (1978). *Dictionary of gaming, modeling and simulation.* Beverly Hills, CA: Sage.

Gredler, M. (1992). *Designing and evaluating games and simulations: A process approach.* London: Kogan Page.

Greenblat, C. S. (1981). Basic concepts and linkages. In C. S. Greenblat & R. D. Duke (Eds.), *Principles and practices of gaming-simulation* (pp. 19–24). Beverly Hills, CA: Sage.

Jones, K. (1985). *Designing your own simulations.* London: Methuen.

Jones, K. (1987). *Simulations: A handbook for teachers and trainers.* London: Kogan Page.

Lederman, L. C. (1984). Debriefing: A critical reexamination of the postexperience analytic process with implications for its effective use. *Simulation & Games, 15,* 415–431.

Mainiero, L. A., & Tromley, C. L. (1989) Labor relations and intergroup conflict. In Mainiero & C.L. Tromley. *Developing Managerial Skills in Organizational Behavior: Exercises, Cases, and Readings* (pp. 308–315) Englewood Cliffs, NJ: Prentice Hall.

McKeachie, W. J. (1994). *Teaching tips: Strategies, research, and theory for college and university teachers.* Lexington, MA: D. C. Heath.

Ruben, B. D., & Lederman, L. C. (1982). Instructional simulation gaming. *Simulation & Games, 13,* 233–244.

Chapter 3

Brookfield, S. D. (1987). *Developing critical thinkers: Challenging adults to explore alternative ways of thinking and acting.* San Francisco: Jossey-Bass.

Burns, A. C., & Gentry, J. W. (1998). Motivating students to engage in experiential learning: A tension-to-learn theory. *Simulation & Gaming, 29,* 133–151.

Cunningham, J. B. (1984). Assumptions underlying the use of different types of simulations. *Simulation & Games, 15,* 213–234.

Greenblat, C. S. (1981). Gaming-simulation and social science: Rewards to the designer. In C. S. Greenblat & R. D. Duke (Eds.), *Principles and practices of gaming-simulation* (pp. 41–46). Beverly Hills, CA: Sage.

Herreid, C. F. 1997/1998, December/January. *Journal of college science teaching,* 6.

Jones, K. (1985). *Designing your own simulations.* London: Methuen.

Jones, K. (1987). *Simulations: A handbook for teachers and trainers.* London: Kogan Page.

Lederman, L. C. (1992). Debriefing: Toward a systematic assessment of theory and practice. *Simulation & Gaming, 23,* 145–160.

Loewenstein, G. (1994). The psychology of curiosity: A review and reinterpretation. *Psychological Bulletin, 116* (1), 75–98.

McKeachie, W. J. (1994). *Teaching tips: Strategies, research, and theory for college and university teachers* (9th ed.). Lexington, MA: D. C. Heath.

Semb, G. B., & Ellis, J. A. (1994, Summer). Knowledge taught in school: What is remembered? *Review of Educational Research, 64*(2), 253–286.

Chapter 4

Duke, R. D., & Greenblat, C. S. (1981). Running games: A guide for game operators. In C. S. Greenblat & R. D. Duke (Eds.), *Principles and practices of gaming-simulation* (pp. 125–137). Beverly Hills, CA: Sage.

Elder, C. D. (1973). Problems in the structure and use of educational simulation. *Sociology of Education, 46,* 335–354.

Jones, K. (1985). *Designing your own simulations.* London: Methuen.

Jones, K. (1987). *Simulations: A handbook for teachers and trainers.* London: Kogan Page.

Jones, K. (1988). *Interactive learning events: A guide for facilitators.* London: Kogan Page.

Parente, D. H. (1995). A large-scale simulation for teaching business strategy. In D. Crookall & K. Arai (Eds.), *Simulation and gaming across disciplines and cultures* (pp. 75–82). Thousand Oaks, CA: Sage.

Chapter 5

Bransford, J. D., Brown, A. L., & Cocking, R. R. (2000). *How people learn: Brain, mind, experience, and school.* Washington, DC: National Academy Press.

Brookfield, S. D. (2002). Teaching through discussion as the exercise of disciplinary power. In D. Lieberman (Ed.), *To improve the academy: Resources for faculty, instructional, and organizational development, 20,* 260–273. Bolton, MA: Anker Publishing.

Brookfield S. D., & Preskill, S. (1999). *Discussion as a way of teaching: Tools and techniques for democratic classrooms.* San Francisco: Jossey-Bass.

Costa & O'Leary. (1992). Co-cognition: The cooperative development of the intellect. In N. Davidson & T. Worsham (Eds.), *Enhancing thinking through cooperative learning.* New York: Teachers College.

Crookall, D. (1992). (Editorial) Debriefing. *Simulation & Gaming, 23,* 141–142.

Fulwiler, T. (1987). *Teaching with writing*. Portsmouth, NH: Boynton/Cook.

Leamnson, R. (1999). *Thinking about teaching and learning: Developing habits of learning with first year college and university students*. Sterling, VA: Stylus Press.

Lederman, L. C. (1984). Debriefing: A critical reexamination of the postexperience analytic process with implications for its effective use. *Simulation & Games, 15,* 415–431.

Lederman, L. C. (1992). Debriefing: Toward a systematic assessment of theory and practice. *Simulation & Gaming, 23,* 145–160.

Lowman, J. (1984). *Mastering the techniques of teaching*. San Francisco: Jossey-Bass.

Mainiero, L.A., & Tromley, C. L (1989). Power lab. In L. A. Mainiero & C. L. Tromley. *Developing Managerial Skills in Organizational Behavior: Exercises, Cases, and Readings* (pp. 261–264). Englewood Cliffs, NJ, Prentice Hall.

Palmer, P. (1998). *The courage to teach: Exploring the inner landscape of a teacher's life*. San Francisco: Jossey-Bass.

Steinwach, B. (1992). How to facilitate a debriefing. *Simulation & Gaming, 23,* 186–195.

Thatcher, D. C. (1990). Promoting learning through games and simulations. *Simulation & Gaming, 21,* 262–273.

Thiagarajan, S. (1992). Using games for debriefing. *Simulation & Gaming, 23,* 161–173.

Chapter 6

Angelo, T. A., & Cross, K. P. (1993). *Classroom assessment techniques: A handbook for college teachers* (2nd ed.). San Francisco: Jossey-Bass.

Astin, A. W., Banta, T. W., Cross, K. P., El-Khawas, E., Ewell, P. T., Hutchings, P., Marchese, T. J., McClenny, K. M., Mentkowski, M., Miller, M. A., Moran, E. T., & Wright, B. D. (1992). *Principles of good practice for assessing student learning*. Washington, DC: American Association of Higher Education.

Boyer, E. L. (1990). *Scholarship reconsidered: Priorities of the professoriate.* Princeton, NJ: Carnegie Foundation for the Advancement of Teaching.

Bransford, J. D., Brown, A. L., & Cocking, R. R. (Eds). (2000). *How people learn: Brain, mind, experience, and school.* Commission on Behavioral and Social Sciences and Education National Research Council. Washington, DC: National Academy Press.

Chance, P. (1992, November). The rewards of learning. *Phi Delta Kappa,* 200–207. (Reprinted in *Educational Psychology 97/98 annual editions,* pp. 117–121, 1997/1998, Guilford, CT: Duskin/McGraw-Hill).

Deep learning, surface learning. (1993). *AAHE Bulletin, 45*(8), 14–17.

Duffy, D. K., & Jones, J. W. (1995). *Teaching within the rhythms of the semester.* San Francisco: Jossey-Bass.

Hobson, E. H. (1998). Designing and grading written assignments. In R. S. Anderson & B. W. Speck (Eds.), *Changing the way we grade student performance: Classroom assessment and the new learning paradigm.* New Directions for Teaching and Learning, no. 74 (pp. 51–57). San Francisco: Jossey-Bass.

Jacobs, L. C., & Chase, C. I. (1992). *Developing and using tests effectively: A guide for faculty.* San Francisco: Jossey-Bass.

Kohn, A. (1993, June). Rewards versus learning: A response to Paul Chance. *Phi Delta Kappa,* 783–787. (Reprinted in *Educational Psychology 97/98 annual editions,* 1997/1998, pp. 122–125, Guilford, CT: Duskin/McGraw-Hill)

Lowman, J. (1984). *Mastering the techniques of teaching.* San Francisco: Jossey-Bass.

McKeachie, W. J. (1994). *Teaching tips: Strategies, research, and theory for college and university teachers* (9th ed.). Lexington, MA: D. C. Heath.

Millis, B. J. (1992). Conducting effective peer classroom observations. In D. H. Wulff & J. D. Nyquist (Eds.), *To improve the academy: Resources for faculty, instructional, and organizational development* (pp. 189–201). Stillwater, OK: New Forums Press.

Millis, B. J., & Cottell, P. G (1998). *Cooperative learning for higher education faculty.* Phoenix, AZ: Oryx Press [Now distributed through Greenwood Press].

Nilson, L. B. (1998). *Teaching at its best: A research-based resource for college instructors.* Bolton, MA: Anker Publishing.

Pollio, H. R., & Humphreys, W. L. (1990). Grading students. In M. Weimer & R. A. Neff (Eds.), *Teaching college: Collected readings for the new instructor* (pp. 109–116). Madison, WI: Magna.

Rhem, J. (1995). Deep/surface approaches to learning: An introduction. *The National Teaching & Learning Forum,* 5(1), 1–3.

Speck, B. W. (1998). Unveiling some of the mystery of professional judgment in the classroom. In R. S. Anderson & B. W. Speck (Eds.), *Changing the way we grade student performance: Classroom assessment and the new learning paradigm.* New Directions for Teaching and Learning, no. 74 (pp. 17–31). San Francisco: Jossey-Bass.

Walvoord, B. E., & Anderson, V. J. (1998). *Effective grading: A tool for learning and assessment.* San Francisco: Jossey-Bass.

Woods, D. R. (1994). *Problem-based learning: How to gain the most from PBL.* Waterdown, ON: Donald R. Woods.

Woods, D. R. (1996). *Instructor's guide for problem-based learning: How to gain the most from PBL* (3rd ed.). Retrieved January 14, 1997, from http://chemeng.mcmaster.ca/pbl/pbl.htm [URL verified October 23, 2001.]